SENDING YOUR MILLENNIAL TO COLLEGE

Sending Your Millennial to College

A Parent's Guide to
Supporting College Success

A companion to
Dean's List: 10 Strategies for College Success

JOHN BADER

Johns Hopkins University Press

Baltimore

9 8 7 6 5 4 3 2 1

Johns Hopkins University Press
2715 North Charles Street
Baltimore, Maryland 21218-4363
www.press.jhu.edu

Library of Congress Cataloging-in-Publication Data

Names: Bader, John B., author.
Title: Sending your millennial to college : a parent's guide to supporting
    college success / John Bader.
Description: Baltimore : Johns Hopkins University Press, [2018] | Includes
    bibliographical references and index.
Identifiers: LCCN 2017046660| ISBN 9781421425825 (pbk. : alk. paper) | ISBN
    9781421425832 (electronic) | ISBN 1421425823 (pbk. : alk. paper) | ISBN
    1421425831 (electronic)
Subjects: LCSH: College student orientation. | Generation Y—Education
    (Higher) | Education, Higher—Parent participation.
Classification: LCC LB2343.3 B34 2018 | DDC 378.1/98—dc23
LC record available at https://lccn.loc.gov/2017046660

A catalog record for this book is available from the British Library.

*Special discounts are available for bulk purchases of this book. For more information, please contact
Special Sales at 410-516-6936 or specialsales@press.jhu.edu.*

Johns Hopkins University Press uses environmentally friendly book materials, including recycled
text paper that is composed of at least 30 percent post-consumer waste, whenever possible.

To my late parents, Bill and Gretta Bader

CONTENTS

ACKNOWLEDGMENTS

....

This little book began as a conversation with Greg Britton, of Johns Hopkins University Press, as we discussed the second edition of *Dean's List: 10 Strategies for College Success*. Since leaving Hopkins as a dean, I had worked for organizations focused on K–12 education, and I had learned much about parent-student dynamics. More directly, I then was the parent of a student heading to college, and my perspective had shifted on the role parents could play in college life.

Dean's List now reflects those lessons in its second edition, but I wanted to create a parent's guidebook to serve as a concrete bridge between students and their parents. I wanted to address parents directly, encouraging them to have healthy conversations with their children in college. The book you hold is the result, and I want to thank Greg for encouraging the project and his team for nurturing it from draft to publication and helping it find you.

This guidebook owes much to the same cast of characters as *Dean's List* does, primarily my colleagues at Johns Hopkins University. I want to highlight two of those people, Dan Weiss and Paula Burger. Both of them helped me to grow as a leader and as a person, and they encouraged me to reflect, to write, and to publish on the challenges my advisor colleagues and I faced every day.

I have tried not to embarrass my older son, Calvin, now at Dickinson College, with too many stories found in the following pages. If I have, too bad. His younger brother, Eli, is happy to be exempt. For now. As always, I am grateful for the love and support of my wife, Amy.

I have written most of this guidebook in my early tenure as executive director of the Fulbright Association, the official alumni organization of the scholarship. I appreciate the support of my colleagues Shaz Akram, Michelle Dimino, Kelsey Poholsky, and Alison Aadland. The association's board of directors, led by Nancy Neill, is helping me to thrive in a gracious and innovative atmosphere.

I am lucky to be serving a community that means so much to my family. I was a Fulbrighter to India, as was my father to West Germany. My parents, who were Pomona College classmates, married while on that Fulbright to Germany, and they lived an international life committed to public service and the fine arts. They encouraged my siblings and me to experiment, to travel, to learn, and to serve. They let me choose my own college, my course of study, and my life beyond—knowing that I wasn't always making good choices. I miss them very much, and I dedicate this guidebook on parenting to them.

SENDING YOUR MILLENNIAL TO COLLEGE

Piloting Your Helicopter

It would have been a quiet summer day. Summer, yes. But quiet, no. My wife and I, along with our younger son, watched in awed silence as the Dickinson College campus in Carlisle, Pennsylvania, swirled around us. College campuses have two moments of stunning optimism: the day the freshmen move in and the day the seniors all graduate. We were on a quiet island, witnessing that incoming student migration, a moment of excitement, possibility, wistfulness, and fear.

All around, there was the ordered chaos of getting keys, making beds, finding bathrooms, meeting roommates, identifying landmarks, grabbing food, and wondering what to do next. Having worked on a campus much like Dickinson, I expected this, and I smiled, sensing the familiar anxieties felt by each generational wave of students as they wash ashore on a campus.

What I did not expect were my own feelings. Of course, I had known this day was coming, when we would take our older son to college. My wife and I had braced ourselves for the pain of separation, for the worries about whether he would be happy, for the uncertainties of his independent life, and for the redefinition of our lives without him home every day.

But I didn't expect to feel left out. As the three of us watched, our college freshman helped his new dorm-mate from China get the right room key. He figured out where to get his picture taken for his ID card. He told us where the pre-orientation program meeting was, and we followed him dumbly. We stood outside the crowded meeting room, where he learned where to meet the students he would join to spend three days rock climbing.

And then he said, "OK, *it's time for me to go.*"

What? Wait a minute. This is it? You're going? My brain and my heart just stopped. This is the moment? I struggled to realize what was happening, as my wife took pictures of our sons hugging each other, and as we four folded one another into a family embrace. But I felt like I was floating, unclear and uncertain. Weird, really. I was disconnected, left out, undefined. Sad, as expected, but what were all these other feelings?

And then he was gone. I stumbled toward the car, vaguely aware of the importance of this moment. It's a wonder I didn't drive us off the road on the way home. There wasn't a lot to say during that drive, but plenty to think about, starting with how I was supposed to change as a father. How much was I supposed to let go? What role was I going to play now? How much trust do I have that he will make good choices?

I have been an educator, professor, dean, and administrator nearly all of my professional life. I have given a lot of thought, based on those years of experience, to what my son and students like him need to do to succeed. Those lessons can be found in *Dean's List: 10 Strategies for College Success,* which anchors this companion guide. So, on that summer day, I had a good idea of what my son should do. But I wasn't really sure what I should be doing.

That is why I offer you this modest guide to parenting a successful college student. I needed a way to process my new role, and I think you will find the thoughts, suggestions, and strategies found here to be useful. This guide flies next to *Dean's List,* which is written for your daughter or son, stealing liberally from it in a way that takes a parent's perspective. (I'm relieved to know you can't plagiarize yourself.) That is why the 10 strategies for parenting parallel those that your child could follow in the *Dean's List* version.

I do this intentionally, of course, because the most important result of these books is to provoke serious, sustained, and substantive conversations between you and your student. *Dean's List* and this companion guide, then, need to have similarities in structure, vocabulary, and message that allow those conversations to have a common starting point. I don't want to get in the way of healthy conversations; I want to encourage them, which is why each chapter ends with suggested topics for "Around the Kitchen Table." Don't use them verbatim. That's too self-conscious and off-putting. Reframe them to your needs, voice, and experience, such as whether you attended a US college and whether other children of yours have left for college.

These conversations can and should start before you face a similarly weird moment of goodbyes on some college campus. But you'll likely find, as I have, that you need to keep recalibrating after that, adjusting to new needs as the year progresses. Of course, you're welcome to read this guide all at once, made easier by my efforts to be brief and respectful of your limited time. But remember that not all issues happen at once. It's really OK to postpone worries about failure when you're focused on encouraging your student to experiment and explore. I will discuss how these two concepts are connected, but you do not have to digest it all in one bite.

There is one exception to this rule. Right now, you should consider that parenting a college student is not the same as parenting a high school student. Dropping off a child at college feels momentous because it *is* momentous, a moment when the poles on your compass can and should shift. While this guide and *Dean's List* seek to spark conversation, at the very least, this guide should prompt you to be more self-aware of your changing role and the strategies you can consider.

The principal shift is the realization that your son or daughter needs to learn how to make important decisions *independently*, logically shrinking the role you play in those decisions. You will be seized with doubt by this shift, deeply tempted to intervene, to solve, and to protect. Your elemental role in their lives, of course, has been responsible for their health, well-being, and intellectual growth—their preparation for college and for life. But playing that role well can obscure our ultimate role anchored in our biology—to let go. Why help them prepare if you're unwilling to let them test that preparation?

As we march through 10 strategies of parenting successful students, you will see that letting go is as practical as it is inevitable. But that doesn't make it emotionally easy. Those strategies are designed, then, to help you support a process that helps you become less important—one of the painful ironies of parenting. The hovering parents of college students, the *helicopters*, get a lot of attention. They are the subject of legend among college faculty who are appalled to get a call from a parent disputing their son's test score. In fact, few faculty have these direct encounters. They're more worried by the threat of getting such a call, which is how it became legend among faculty and administrative circles. My favorite urban legend around helicopter parents is the story of a mother accompanying her son to a job interview.

These stories resonate because they reflect an apparent shift in the nature of parent-student relations. This current Millennial generation values a relationship that is open, interdependent, and highly consultative, aided by ever-innovating communications technologies. The deeper reason for these stories is that letting your children grow up is painful, difficult, and ambiguous. We're not sure how or when to let them make decisions. We can see more clearly than they can the consequences of decision-making. We also know that, if they don't get a chance to fail and choose foolishly, they will never gain their own capacity to make decisions without us.

Therefore, what we need is a way to pilot our hovering helicopter in a healthy way, perhaps with a flight plan that takes us farther away when possible and right to their side when necessary. This book is my attempt to help you pilot your helicopter.

Let's begin with an overview or summary of the 10 strategies to get you started. Then, we will review some of the threads that connect those strategies to one other, such as how different high school and college really are and how that affects your relationship.

Strategy #1: Think about "Why"

Going to college. It's what people do, right? But *why*? Why is the investment worth it? We know it's a stepping-stone, though we may not know to what. Graduate school? Careers? Prestige? All possible. But does it have its own value? The first strategy for parents is to be sure that you and your student are clear on why they are going to college at all. It's hard to measure success if you don't know what it means and worse if you have one set of expectations and your student has another. Here, I'll argue that becoming a *learned person* should define the experience, and I'll discuss how to talk about it.

Strategy #2: Rethink Your Relationship

While this entire guide will push you to rethink your approach to parenting, this chapter will put that relationship in a clear, but harsh, light. What roles should you play? How will those roles change over time? What can you expect from your student, and how can you help them make your relationship more mature and mutually respectful? These questions may be especially challenging to parents who did not attend college, those living outside the United States, and those from traditional cultures. American colleges expect you to keep your distance. How can you do that comfortably?

Strategy #3: Understand Where They Are

Just by being on a campus and paying attention, students can learn more about the institution around them, appreciating the players, their roles, and how to play the system. But you're not there. If you've never spent time on an American campus, you don't even have a starting point. So this strategy, to know the college, is a special challenge, particularly as you feel helpless when your student struggles or has problems. Do I call the president? What's a dean? My son's high school teachers met with me, why won't his professors? Why can't I look at my daughter's transcript when I'm paying the bills? I'll answer those questions here.

Strategy #4: Appreciate Their Academic Choices

You may have thought about what they might learn, provoking them to ask those questions about what is interesting and why, but you may not know all that is before them. And that ignorance will limit your ability to suggest new avenues of exploration, or it may frustrate you when they explore beyond your comfort zone. "No, no. Don't look at *that*. That choice will not get you a job, it won't challenge you, it won't . . ." You become the realist based on a limited view of what is realistic, when there is much more out there. So this strategy will focus on choice and how to encourage unique but informed decisions.

Strategy #5: Disconnect Majors and Careers

This strategy might be in the middle of the list, but it can be an area of deep contention between parents and students. You worry about payoff and jobs. They worry about grades and whether they're bored. They say, "Archaeology," and you say, "Chemistry," when it may be possible to do both. Here, I'll reflect on why, in the United States, there is a disconnect between courses of study or majors and the careers that await. You'll see that majors are poor predictors of professional paths, which may be a familiar story line in your own life. If we see the disconnect, then we can support more freedom—while being mindful of important skills that can get them a job.

Strategy #6: Support How They Work

Among the frustrations you have (or will have) as the parent of a college student is that you have no idea how much or how little they are studying. At home, you had some sense of this, even though they were upstairs and likely taking too many breaks to play games on their phones or to watch Netflix on their iPad. Still, you had visibility and some control. Not anymore. So what can you do about that? What strategies should they be using to study effectively, and how could you influence whether they follow those strategies?

Strategy #7: Invite Them to Be Uncomfortable

This strategy for success will seem counterintuitive. You want your college student to be happy, secure, and safe. You might think of a college campus as a cocoon, where they can grow, protected, into a magnificent creation ready to fly. But that is missing an important mission of American colleges, the desire to challenge them out of their preconceptions, prejudices, and perspectives. A college campus is deliberately diverse to push students to consider and then respect "the other," those who are different than they are. And the university or college wants students to leave campus to experience the wider world on its terms. Your job, fighting all your instincts, is to encourage them to do just that.

Strategy #8: Know the Signs and Reasons for Failure

The most important feature of this guide, and of *Dean's List*, is to confront, openly and honestly, the real (and sometimes realized) possibility of academic failure. Naturally, you don't want this to happen to your son or daughter. But denying the possibility is to avoid important conversations that could either prevent such disasters or help them cope with the fallout. I will discuss the most common factors that cause failure to help you see the early signs. It's also important to know that occasional or chronic failing is common even at the best universities and colleges. So you will not be alone, but you must be prepared—as uncomfortable as that will be.

Strategy #9: Help Them to Forgive Themselves and Rebuild

We all make mistakes. We all make poor choices. We all have problems. The questions are, When faced with mistakes or problems, do we address them directly and confidently? Do we work on them or deny their existence? More critically, do we find a way to forgive ourselves and one another? Your child has been shaped, in part, by how you react to their mistakes, and that will not change when they are in college. With the stakes becoming increasingly high, you will have to make decisions about whether and how to get help for your struggling student. You will choose what tone you will take as you offer (or fail to give) your support. These moments can define your adult relationship with your daughter or son, so you should be self-conscious and mindful as you make those decisions. Do you model and offer forgiveness? Are you open to better paths for them? Can you help them move on?

Strategy #10: Encourage Them to Plan for Life after College

You may be way ahead of your student in thinking about jobs, careers, and life after graduation. Indeed, you may be too far out in front, imagining options they haven't seen yet, setting expectations they won't meet, and drawing plans they will never follow. This is a powerfully dangerous moment as a parent—setting up yourself for failure and setting up your son or daughter for resentment and pushback. You likely have already found that pushing your increasingly independent-minded teenager predictably results in eye-rolling, arms-crossing, and angry eyes that could light the curtains on fire—even when you're right. The consequences intensify when you're talking about early career choices. I'll offer some thoughts on navigating conversations about the future without needing to replace the curtains.

The Big Picture

Marvin Hupart, a favorite high school teacher of mine, always pushed us to see the big picture after every history lesson. He would jump on top of desks, imitating his hero Groucho Marx, and challenge us to pull things together coherently. Here are a few big picture ideas scattered throughout this book.

- *Modesty is important.* Parents are accustomed to being in charge and to knowing what's best. Or, at least, they think they are. But you will have to approach the challenge of a daughter or son in college with a little more modesty and humility. You may not know what you're talking about, to put it bluntly, even if you have attended college or, worse, attended *their* college. You may keep referring to your own experiences, when the landscape might be quite different: new times, new issues, new demands, new problems. You will always be a powerful advisor to your student, but try to hold back the certitude. You might be wrong.
- *They know more than you.* OK. I'm repeating myself, but bear with me. You are not on the campus. You do not see through their eyes. You cannot easily judge mood or sense trouble. You do not walk among the students on their way to class nor sit in a classroom. You do not (really) know where the advising or counseling centers are, and you can't tell how welcoming or helpful they are. So it is possible that they know things, and you don't. This realization may make you more modest, but it should also challenge you to learn what you can. Who are the people in the administration? What can they do for or with you? What resources are available? Don't assume any of this, or that it's the same as you knew in college. And if you did not go to college, or attended college outside the United States, you don't even know where to start. Reading Strategy #3

will help, but make it a goal to learn more about what is happening on campus.

- *College is a lot different than high school.* As your daughter or son has aged through high school, you likely paid less attention to their daily academic experience. You might have been a home-room volunteer in their elementary school, but their high school classrooms have been strictly off limits. And now, you're not even seeing the campus where they live. So you'll have to take it on faith that there are significant differences they must face when moving from one to the other:
  - Professors won't know them and don't think of themselves as teachers.
  - Life is even more unstructured as time in the classroom is cut by two-thirds.
  - The institution is big and difficult to navigate, let alone under-stand.
  - They might think they don't have time to get involved, when they must to stay anchored.
- *You're not there, but your support is crucial.* This is another obvious point but deeply important and a driving idea behind this guide-book. The principal difference with high school is that you're not with them. They have a lot to figure out in that environment: when to go to sleep, what to eat, how to spend their time, what people to befriend, how much discipline to give their studies, how clean to keep themselves and their room. Life is the sum of small decisions like these, and you're not there to affect them. You now become a different kind of life partner—a sounding board, a touchstone, a distant guide. If you need to pick one place to interfere and annoy in this new role, make it their health. Deep sleep, sound nutrition, an active body, and a centered mind are fundamental to college success. Insist that they take care of those things, and the rest will fall in line.
- *How you measure support affects whether you are "successful."* This guidebook and its companion, *Dean's List*, spend a lot of time on this concept. I will argue, again and again, that external measures of success—prestige, grades, professor approval, family pride—set up dynamics that can lead to failure measured the same way.

When students are motivated by external expectations, rather than by internal curiosity and the desire to be learned, they will lose the drive needed to be disciplined, hardworking, and insightful. So, how *you* look at and define success—what feedback you give them as they progress—will have a profound effect on where they get their motivation and how lasting it is.

- *Planning and advice are fleeting.* Any good plan, any good advice, is worth questioning. Your plans or expectations of their experience may be vague ("Do well and have a good time.") or quite specific ("Take Organic Chemistry this year so you can apply to medical school in your junior year."). You may have shared your expectations or just hoped for the best. But know that whatever you're thinking or whatever you've planned, it's likely that it won't work out the way you expected. Your son or daughter is a work in progress, and now that development will be buffeted by factors beyond your control and your reach, which means that plans will change and advice will become outdated. Expect to be surprised, disappointed, baffled, and left out. They are in charge because you're not there.

- *Be ready for failure.* This guidebook will ask you to confront the common reality that students fail. Failure may be momentary—an unexpected poor grade in a crucial subject—or deeply affecting, resulting in probation and suspension. I will outline many intersecting reasons for such failure, as well as ways to cope with them. But you need to expect that such failures don't just happen to other people's children. They will happen to yours. When you're ready for this news, unsurprised, you will be better prepared to offer support, resources, and especially forgiveness. You know this already. If your children see that your love is not tied to success or failure, they can enjoy the risks of a challenging academic environment without the constant fear of losing you and your support.

- *Freedom is a great gift.* I end this list with the most important of these big pictures. We live in an extraordinary era of mobility and choice. It is easy to forget that, not long ago and right now in many parts of the world, young men and especially young women have not had the painful joys that freedom of choice affords. The freedom to pick their academic and professional path is painful because it comes with so many uncertainties. An open landscape is much scarier than one with clear margins and limitations. You may be tempted to create those limitations to ease their worries, but it will deprive them of the rights that you and your family have worked so hard to give them. And you may be doing that mostly to calm your own anxieties, however legitimate they may be. Your daughter or son has chosen the path of an American college, and that path is intentionally open to bring out the best in them. Consider it an act of faith in them and a celebration of the freedom generations have sought to enjoy.

Around the Kitchen Table

After you have let your daughter or son travel to college, you will look around, feeling empty and incomplete. You will stand in their room, picking up odds and ends, rearranging clothes, and wondering what to do with the tall pile of papers left on their now lonely desk. There is a big void in your life, and little solace that the void is caused by a happy—and long-anticipated—departure to college. That college may be a few hours away, which is all that separates our son from my wife and me, or across the planet. You may be counting the days to a fall holiday or lamenting that you can't afford to bring them home or visit them for many months, perhaps the entire year. Not a good moment, as you stand in that room.

But you can take some comfort in remembering the conversation that I hope you have started with him or her. I hope this guide, and *Dean's List*, gives you the topics and vocabulary for that ongoing conversation about what college is about and how to take advantage of it. You're welcome to use some or all of the questions at the end of this section to initiate that conversation. I wished my parents had asked those questions, as the full force of going to college didn't hit me until I was minutes from being dropped off myself many years ago.

But I like to think that my parents were sending me a message by avoiding those questions. They were telling me that my college experience belonged to me and that I could make of it what I liked. I knew they would be there if I failed or needed help, so the more important message was that it was time for me to go.

As you say goodbye, at a bus stop or an airport or standing stupidly on a college campus, know that a great adventure awaits them. You will crave stories from that adventure, even though you can expect very few. And you will begin your own adventure of redefining your role in their lives. I hope this guidebook helps.

* How did you feel when we dropped you off? (Or how do you think you will feel?)
* Before you go, is there anything you're worried about?
* We will really miss you when you're gone. How often should we talk?
* What should we do if you start having a tough time?
* What are some of the specific differences you're seeing from high school? How are you dealing with those differences?
* How are you feeling about the many choices you can make?
* Do you feel like you need a plan to get through all this? Why or why not?

Think about "Why"

As you stand at this moment, watching your daughter or son head for a distant adventure, reflect on their academic career and what you remember about it. Working backward, you just saw them graduate from high school. The look of that ceremony, if there was one, varies across the world, but in the United States, the graduates cover themselves with robes and mortarboards. You are glad, relieved, and proud. Graduation? Done.

High school graduation is the coda to a series of clear accomplishments college-bound students will have. Final examinations? Done with measured scores. Transcript? Done with exacting requirements. That's finished, and her or his GPA is now set. College admissions? Done with a specific list of acceptances—the more prestigious or recognizable, the better. College essays? Done with all the boxes completed. SAT/ACT? Done with more quantitative metrics. You can keep going backward in time, recalling classes taken, AP/IB scores achieved, grades won or lost.

Without paying attention, you have developed the same habit as your student: thinking of academic success as the achievement of measurable outcomes—test scores, grades, and requirements. Admission to a famous university, say, an Ivy League school, such as Princeton or Yale, is the pinnacle of this culture of achievement. That outcome communicates to other parents, family members, and friends that our children are successful. They have hit markers along the way, such as high scores on the SAT, which validate their talents. We are reassured that we have been doing something right as parents.

You're not going to drop that habit just because they are moving on to college. And why would you? Those external measures of success are easy to understand, quick to communicate, and linked to obvious long-run outcomes. Graduate schools and employers will recognize Duke, Stanford, or Brown on a resumé much more readily than Beloit, Ursinus, or Austin—which are profiled in Loren Pope's *Colleges That Change Lives: 40 Colleges That Will Change the Way You Think about Colleges* (New York: Penguin Books, 2012).

Never mind that you can be miserable at Duke and fully engaged in Beloit's dynamic community. But no one is going to argue that a Duke degree has wider name recognition than the little college in Wisconsin. It makes sense to hope that they get admitted to a famous, brand-name school to increase their odds for professional and personal success.

Once they are enrolled in this well-recognized institution, you're likely to continue the related habit of demanding good grades. After all, that's what got your son or daughter into college. Consistent excellence (as measured by good grades), coupled with a university's measurement of rigor (itself an external judgment), fueled their admission experience. Grades determined outcomes, and they will continue to do so. You can't receive C's and expect to be admitted to medical or law school. You know that. I get that.

I also get that college tuition is an investment. When that investment costs more than $60,000 for many private institutions in the United States, there had better be a payoff. You likely are taking on significant debt to finance this experience, perhaps taking out a second mortgage or maxing out credit cards and lines of credit. The financial strain and worry is going to sharpen your need for reassurance that the investment is worth it. And that anxiety will be more effectively allayed if you have a quick and simple way to measure the return on investment—high grades.

This chapter is designed to question that conclusion and to ask, aloud, "Why go to college?" I will argue that Strategy #1 of supporting a successful college student is to *Think about "Why."* Why do we push our children to attend college, to choose a marketable major or course of study, and to get good grades? What is the payoff that we expect and want? Sure, some answers are obvious—get a good job, enjoy a career, and don't move back into your room at home—but is that enough? What are American colleges and universities trying to do when they take in your son or daughter?

I will argue here that you need to rethink how you measure success if you want to see them succeed. There's just no way around this logic. If you look for one outcome and see another, then you cannot say something was a success. You put dough in the oven, expecting it to rise into a light loaf of bread. But it came out flat and dense. If you keep an open mind, you might appreciate that a dense bread can be richly flavorful and filling. But if you picture the "right" way that bread should taste, then you will be disappointed. Your child is already different from what you imagined them to be when they were much younger. Is it time to rethink whether you are proud or disappointed? I think so.

Consider instead a student-centered measure of success, independent of grades and external approval. Have they been fulfilled and challenged by their education? Have they come to see new perspectives, to appreciate the complexity of the cosmos and the beauty of poetry and painting? Do they see the cultural complexities of Japan and China? Do they have the tools to make sense of the world around them and then to communicate their findings with clarity, evidence, and conviction? Sure, they might get good grades if they do all of this well, but that's not the point, and it's not enduring either. Long after they have forgotten their grades, they will carry the confidence of an intellectual explorer and the self-respect of someone who loves that the world is complicated and beyond full understanding.

Whether they allow themselves to measure their success that way will depend, to a large degree, on you. Your value system is part of their cognitive and emotional DNA already, like it or not. Your influence on their sense of self and confidence remains profound. You can help realign their view of success and the educational mission they have begun, or you can be an obstacle to that. You can encourage them to explore. You can walk gently around the subject of grades. Or you can reinforce old habits by showing your disappointment, even subtly, when those grades and course selections do not align with your hopes.

The choice is yours, of course. But when you re-engineer the definition of success, you help create the incentive to enjoy a college education on its own terms. If you are open to less quantitative measures, you will help make that education an enduring, positive mark on their lives.

The Challenges of Grading

Grades, or marks, are a practical, elegant solution to a problem. How do we hold students accountable? We are motivated by need and by want, of course. So we have created an incentive system for students to learn by holding them accountable for their mastery by grading them.

This makes a lot of sense. Learning, particularly in a classroom setting, does not have easy alternatives. Grades create a sense of urgency. They tap into our natural and learned competitive culture. They are without expense, as awarding an A is as free as an F. They create a power system for instruction, giving teachers and professors the authority to make a quiet, serious, and focused learning environment. Students may earn their grades, but instructors have the power to determine whether something has been "earned." By handing out good grades to some, but not to others, instructors create a hierarchy of obedience and approval. Some students have pleased us, others have not. The former group gets A's, the latter does not.

Grading has a practical elegance, as well. Grades allow individuals and institutions who do not know a student to pass judgment on his or her worth or potential. We can compare one student's average with another's, if we must choose between them. We then can hand out awards, scholarships, commendations, and admissions to measurably "successful" students and not to others. We can't give everything to everyone, of course, and we know that not everyone does as well as everyone else. So a system that creates incentives to learn, supports an instructional hierarchy, and enables decision-making is an effective system. No wonder it dominates education.

But there are serious, significant consequences to keeping grading at the center of educational identity and measures of success. First, it is an emotional minefield. As I note in *Dean's List*, the moment students get back an exam, a paper, or an assignment, they quickly and anxiously look at the grade or mark. If it is an A, they are flooded with relief and pride, as if they held their breath between completing the assignment and receiving its mark. If it is anything else, they likely will be disappointed, confused, and even ashamed.

While these feelings are understandable, as a parent, you need to wonder whether this system is emotionally abusive. We must all learn to cope with feedback, constructive or not, and accepting grades is an important part of that life lesson. But it creates emotional complexity and contradictions at a moment when the student needs to take stock of what they have learned, what value their work has added, and what strength they have drawn from the experience. The emotional roller coaster of grades makes that more difficult.

Second, grades can obscure an appreciation for what students learn, which builds on the point I just made. Consider the disappointment of a B. B's are awarded to students who understand the material, have learned to apply it, and exhibit an appreciation of the subject matter. They are good, solid students. But because they have not reached some preconceived notion of excellence or have made a few mistakes, their mark is a little lower. This creates a veil over something more important: they have learned something. Indeed, they have learned it well, and it has transformed them in some way. Yet the emotional reaction is disappointment when it should be celebration.

Third, by giving instructors the power to grade, we put them at the center of learning. To thrive in a graded system, the smart student figures out what would please the instructor. Canny students do this intuitively and strategically, looking at any cues the teacher or professor offers on what would make them happy. Again, there is a life lesson here. As a practical matter, we need to know what our supervisors want from us in our professional lives in order to remain employed and advance.

But this may be conceding more power to instructors than we should. Students, looking to please them, will fail to look for pleasures and discoveries in the subject matter. Instead, they look to meet the immediate needs of instructors. They won't head down a path of curiosity because, if they want a good grade, that curiosity would be a waste of time.

And then what happens when students graduate, and there are no more instructors? Do they give up on learning? That would be both a shame and a professional mistake in an ever-changing employment landscape. You have to find motivation from within to push forward, and waiting for the approval of an absent instructor will be your undoing.

Finally, grades create a zero-sum game in which there must be as many losers as winners. This generation may be mocked for winning a trophy just for participating. "Everyone is a winner" sounds silly and is enabling. Still, learning and academics are not the same as competition, athletic or otherwise. Learning is always an additive experience. You can learn a little or a lot, but it is hard to unlearn, so there is value to any educational moment.

But grades suggest otherwise. Some students will get good grades, and others won't. A grading curve, used commonly in math and the sciences, predetermines that students will perform in a distributed way, on a curve, so there have to be winners and losers. I'm not denying that students will vary in performance and that a curve may reflect that reality. But in expecting varying outcomes, in judging one over another, we create the "loser" mentality in those that fall short or fail. And that compounds the emotional minefield.

Where does this leave us? I'm not suggesting that you entirely ignore grades.* That's just not practical. There are too many benefits to good grades. And it's unrealistic to undo an incentive system that has worked for your son or daughter and has been helpful to you to track their progress. But you need to realize that grades create unhealthy incentives, that they have unintended consequences, and that they deflect attention from the real benefits of a college education—the real payoff of becoming a learned person.

*Getting access to your son's or daughter's grades will not be as easy as it was when they were in high school. American higher education has a legal wall around it, imposed by FERPA (Family Educational Rights and Privacy Act). Colleges are obligated to share information, including grades, only with students, as their central relationship. While you may be paying the tuition bills, this does not mean you are recognized as a player. Many parents object to this, but it is a futile objection. You simply will not know what is going on, including what grades your child has earned, without (a) asking your student or (b) having them sign a waiver (provided by the college or university) that gives you that access. I caution you against pushing for this waiver, unless your student has serious health concerns, such as depression, or has other challenges. You need to respect their privacy and independence, as this entire guidebook argues.

Another Way to Measure Success

If we set aside the achievement of good grades as the driving goal in college, or at least keep it limited and in perspective, there are other ways to measure success. Some of these, such as acquiring key analytic and communication skills, will be discussed in later chapters. Others might be more personal, such as making lasting friendships or enjoying romance and love. Your daughter or son might be a serious athlete, so they dream of championships, a musician hoping to master a Chopin concerto, or an artist gathering works for an attention-grabbing show.

Here, I propose a goal that every college student should make his or her highest academic priority: *to become learned.* "Learned" may have an old-fashioned feel to it. But I choose it intentionally to connect the modern college experience with an attitude held since at least the Enlightenment that contentment and achievement begin with a wide understanding of the world and the people in it. You can help your son or daughter think about this lofty but important goal because you have the perspective and experience they lack to see its value. You know that the world after college will be complex and shifting, that an integrated global economy awaits them, and that it is not enough to see one dimension of life when there is time to savor so many wide-ranging experiences.

If you choose to support this approach to the opportunity ahead, you will be sending a message consistent with most US universities and colleges. These institutions have given great thought to the meaning of "learned," a concept that will underpin their curricula policies and choices. Some universities, such as Columbia, will outline specific courses all undergraduates must take to be learned in the way their faculty holds dear. Others will demand that their students spread themselves widely, filling "distribution" or "general education" requirements, because they insist that learned means intellectual diversity. They want students to respect many disciplines, to see connections between them, and to gather information as widely as they can manage.

There is a historic reason for this, in part. The United States was founded in a sparsely populated wilderness. The traditions and contributions of the native peoples were either overlooked or ignored. So they felt it necessary to build a wholly new polity, a citizenry that could engage with and govern one other. And that led many communities, faiths, and peoples to found colleges and universities as fundamental to such a polity. In keeping with Western cultural traditions, particularly those of the Enlightenment, that meant a broad education to build a skeptical, engaged citizenry, not a specialized workforce.

It is crucial that, as a parent, you understand this as a fundamental, driving idea in the American academy. If you are paying the bills, then you are paying faculty and staff to do their best in promoting this concept, that a liberal education must be broad and varied to nurture learned people. If you're thinking that expertise or marketable credentials are the outcome, you will be disappointed or frustrated.

The good news is that this educational system is anchored in choice, which means your daughter or son can make choices that build their own definition of learned. Even the most proscribed curriculum will allow plenty of room for choosing tailored pathways. You can think of your role as encouraging the discovery of that pathway. Ask them what they want to learn, where their curiosities lie, and what puzzles they would like to solve. A college may offer direction or requirements to mandate such exploration, but the student really has ownership of what being learned means.

What do you want to learn? It seems like a simple question, but it is rarely posed. You could be the unusual parent who does. If that question dead ends with "I don't know," keep pushing. What was interesting to you in high school? What are you reading that feeds you exciting ideas? Remember the trip we took to ____? What questions came from that trip that you remember?

You can be more specific, if you like. A look at recent headlines would spark conversation. How do Americans elect their leaders? Is there need for reform in this process? What is the science behind climate change? What has been the role of Russia and Western allies in Syria? What are the causes of mass migration, and what have governments done about that?

Think more broadly than that. What are the artistic and musical traditions of South Africa? What are the elements of a Brahms symphony? What are the chemical properties of gasoline that power engines and pollute the air? How does an iPhone work? What are the defining features of your favorite movies that make it so memorable?

A conversation like this might seem odd or forced, depending on the kinds of things you usually talk about. But asking your college student about what they want to learn will have a powerful impact on how they view the opportunity, and even how they see you. They may have obsessed about grades in high school, with little regard to what they have learned, and you may be partly responsible for that.

If you never discussed what they learned, only keeping an eye on grades, then they will be surprised to get these questions from you. They may not be able to answer them, partly because it's hard to know what you don't know. But it will be clear that you want them to think about those questions, that you value what they want to and can learn. If you understand the journey they are on, why not encourage a new way of thinking of its success?

Around the Kitchen Table

I hope this chapter has challenged you to think about your own expectations for your daughter or son as they begin college. You may not be conscious of the reward and incentive system that grading creates and how that can run counter to wider educational and social goals for a higher education. I don't blame you at all. We all live in cultures where external expectations play a determining role in our lives. The question is what power we give to those expectations and whether we can add a richer dimension based on what we can mean by being learned.

If you get stuck on grades and credentials, you are not serving your son or daughter well. You will not have a sense of process or mission. You will not appreciate the complexity and opportunity of their experience. You will focus them on outcomes determined by others. While that may be practical, it can be empty and a weak motivator for climbing the mountain looming before them.

If you hope they become learned and encourage a conversation around what that means, you will be supporting success in a way that cannot fail. If you broaden the conversation and push it to wonder aloud what is worth knowing and understanding, you will be doing something your son or daughter will struggle to do on their own. You will help them figure out what they want from the time, energy, investment, and hard work of a college education.

If you broaden the payoff to include being learned, sophisticated, tolerant, and insightful, then the payoff will be rich and enduring. And that thought will be very comforting, as you stand in their empty bedroom and wonder if they're doing OK.

* How will you know if you're doing well in college?
* When you were in high school, what did it feel like to get a poor grade? What did you think a poor grade was?
* How did I react when you told me news about your grades or when I looked at your report card?
* Would you have preferred I reacted differently? Or didn't ask you at all?
* How should we handle news about your college grades?
* What do you think is the reason to go to college at all? Are there other reasons you can name?
* What will make you think that you are getting what you want out of it?
* What do you want to learn while you're there? How can you make that happen?

Rethink Your Relationship

O ne morning in December while my older son was a freshman, I ran into a neighbor while I was walking the dog. "I'm going to pick him up from Dickinson this morning," I said. "I wonder if we can all stand each other for the month that he's home."

She just smiled. "Oh, I remember in August when you were a basket case. You were unhappy, missing him terribly, wondering how life would be like without him. And here you are, wondering if he's going to mess that up!"

I had to admit things had changed. In the first days after he left, I had to restrain myself from calling or texting—or both—every day. I worried about his new classes, whether he would get along with his roommate, how he would make friends, whether he had chosen the right college. On and on. I kept saying to myself, "You've literally written the book on this, telling parents to let them grow and decide independently. Yet you keep reaching for that phone, you hypocrite." Yep, caught in the act.

My neighbor was right, too. In only a few months, I had begun to act with more restraint and sanity. I thought I had internalized my own advice, only to find how difficult it was to follow. Still, I was doing better with the passage of time. The longer it passed, the more restraint I showed. That does not mean I didn't interfere—"Have you talked to the Career Center about internships this winter or summer?" I kept asking—but it did mean I found some balance and perspective.

This chapter, like its parallel in *Dean's List*, explores directly the changing nature of your relationship with your college daughter or son. Issues of this relationship animate this entire guidebook, of course. But I offer Strategy #2 for success, *Rethink Your Relationship*, by discussing how important it is to create more space between you and your son or daughter. I have just confessed that this is not easy advice to follow; I am still figuring out how to do this myself. I acknowledge that many traditional cultures would dispute the wisdom of such advice, which may fly in the face of their values and expectations. Still, creating space or distance between you is a mission worth embracing, as the payoff will far exceed the effort.

How do I know this? Because I have seen too many cases in which parents, by reason of habit or unchecked anxiety, do not adapt to life separated from their college son or daughter. They insist on remaining in control of decisions and choices. They need constant feedback and engagement, perhaps to reassure themselves of a familiar role or to validate their parenting. They may travel across the world to campus or simply pick up the phone, but their intent is the same: remain in charge. And they have earned the name *helicopter parents* for hovering too closely and too long.

The costs of that approach are significant, damaging, and immediate. Students with inseparable parents choose courses and majors to please or obey their parents, rather than to satisfy their curiosity or intellectual growth. Their learning is burdened, sometimes tragically, by resentment and anger. Unable to do what they want, they do not do the hard work required of excellence. They hope that passive aggression in the form of failed coursework will send the message: *leave me alone.*

In the Strategy #1 chapter, I argued that students need to own their education by deciding what is worth learning. Pursuing good grades for their own sake is a form of surrendering ownership to the instructor. Please instructors, follow their path, obey their standards, and you'll get good grades. But students who do this will have forgotten that the learning belongs to them. Parents who insist on making decisions are playing the same role, depriving the student of ownership and the motivation for excellence that comes with it.

This means the stakes are high for you to adapt to this new world of real, perceived, and growing independence. The high stakes may help you see the urgency, but they will not make it easy. There is no smooth glide path to independence for any student, as I have discovered as an inconsistent parent myself. And there are many good reasons to remain gently but insistently engaged—to be sure they are healthy, that they are thinking ahead, that they know you will support them if they fail. But I can assure you that it's worth the effort.

Taking Stock

At a moment of reflection like this, it is wise to take stock of your relationship with your son or daughter. If there is a scale of involvement/interference, from indifference to helicopter, where are you? You can build that scale based on your answers to a list of questions, though you're welcome to come up with your own list:

- *What was your role in their college application?* Time for a confessional. How many of the colleges that your daughter applied to did *you* choose? Did you laugh or scoff at ideas your son floated? Did you schedule them for SAT prep courses or tutoring? How many times did you push them to take the ACT? Did they write all the essays themselves or did you "suggest" prose? These are not easy questions to answer for anyone, especially when your intentions— to get them into a great college or university—are laudable, even if your methods might have been a bit aggressive. The college admission process can give you a starting point for the decision-making dynamic in your family, and the relative strength of your role and your son's or daughter's.

- *How closely did you monitor their grades in high school?* You know the stakes of good grades or marks. If there's a pattern of under-achievement there, dreams of Harvard or Stanford become more remote. Or that's what you're thinking! How much did this thought trouble you? What did you do about it? How often did you ask your student what grade they got on one test or another? Did you constantly check the school's online system for grades? Did that intelligence spur you to action, insisting on tutoring or calling a teacher to demand an explanation or extra credit? You likely struggled with what was the right thing to do. You know your limitations and the politics of parent-faculty relations, and you have an instinctive role to defend your child. I'm not judging you here, as I know how you feel. I'm only asking where you are on the anxiety/action scale of grades.

- *How much pushing did you do to get them to practice or study?* How much interference on your part did it take to get them to practice an instrument, condition themselves for a sport, or complete their homework? How many times a day did you tell them to turn off their iPad, put down their phone, lower the volume on their Beats headphones, and get to work? There is no right answer, though it shouldn't have been "never." Face it, kids lack focus. Practicing and studying are not fun. Who doesn't need discipline imposed on them, especially children? But you can question how forceful you were and whether that now looks overly aggressive. More importantly, it gives you a baseline for how much pushing you will do from a distance, and how much trust you have that they will do the work needed to do well in college.

- *How much contact do you now maintain?* I have already confessed that, in the first months of my son's life in college, I was guilty of reaching out too much. I was tempted to text every day. Our rule to speak only on Sundays proved a difficult one to follow. Millennials like your daughter or son are famous for their friend-like relationship with their parents and so the normal habit of communicating constantly. Certainly, that's helpful and loving at some level. Now you need to take stock of what you are doing. How often do you call, text, FaceTime, Skype, or e-mail?

- *What role did you play in picking their first set of college classes?* The summer before freshman year is confusing and fast-paced. The college or university keeps sending you more and more material, with deadlines, reminders, instructions, and demands. Fill out a roommate questionnaire. Order bed linens. Pay your tuition bill. But the one that may be the most daunting, with the highest impact, is picking classes. The college or university will offer help with course selection, no doubt, coming from a faculty member or academic advisor. (Use that help.) The question here is how much of a role did *you* play in picking those classes? Did you keep using *we* as a pronoun, as in "We need to take Calculus and Chemistry right away." This first year sets several important habits, among them how classes are chosen. How aggressively did you express your concerns, preferences, and needs?

- *How much of a plan have you made for them?* Picking courses, of course, may be part of a plan. Maybe that's a plan to be a pre-med, preparing for medical school. Maybe it's dreams of being a lawyer, financial genius, or chemical engineer. Perhaps it's less specific professionally but more focused academically, such as thinking of the utility of the sciences, statistics, or economics. How deeply embedded is this plan in your family conversations and decisions? Did it affect where they applied to college? How long have you had this plan? How jointly owned with your son or daughter is it? Did it come from you or from them? How has it grown, say, with volunteerism or summer programs? The answer to these questions will give you a read for the expectations your student will take with them, and how flexible you are on what they do. They also set a baseline for how strong a role you play in long-term planning, a habit that may be hard to modify or undo.

- *What would you think or do if they don't follow that plan?* When things have not gone according to plan in the past—they don't like playing piano so refuse more lessons, they don't have the self-discipline or talent to stick with ballet or tennis, they take no pleasure in volunteering—how have you coped with that? Here, of course, I'm asking that you get a sense of your flexibility and the degree to which you push back on decisions your son or daughter makes. Sometimes, that pushback is necessary. "Don't give up on piano. You may be a little bored after years of lessons, but you're really good at it, and you'll enjoy it all your life. How about we get a different teacher so you can focus on pop music?" Sometimes, though, you have to surrender. There's no manual for how that works. It's just one of the many challenges of being a parent. Again, I'm not looking to judge how flexible you are, just to focus your attention on where you are, and seeing how challenging it will be to adapt to your new life as a college parent.

There is no science to this scale, any more than there is a correct place to be on this scale—though both Aristotle and I would not recommend the two far ends. (Aristotle did not care for extremes.) If you ask yourself these questions, you will begin to get a feel for where you are and what habits you will maintain, modify, or break. Consider this the starting point of a glide path, gentle or steep, to moving toward greater independence for your son or daughter. The movement does not have to be large, as you may need to experiment and move cautiously if this is a new concept.

Understand, though, that you need to move forward on this glide path to help them succeed in the short run and become fully functional adults in the long run. Moving in that direction is not an act of indifference but of love. You need to find a path that gives you room to show your concern and love, engages you when you are most needed, but gives them the opportunity to make and learn from mistakes. In effect, I'm not suggesting you change your motivations—to be sure they are happy, successful, and healthy—but your methods.

What You *Can* Do

It might be easier to do this if we start with what role you should clearly play. Where are you most needed? (Then we'll look at where you need to back off.) Let's start with the obvious. You need to be sure they are healthy. As you will see in other chapters, both here and in *Dean's List*, health issues are fundamental to academic success. Students are at risk if they do not eat well, if they get insufficient exercise, and especially if they fail to get enough sleep.

Yet many students fail on these basics. They gain weight. They lose energy. They stay up until 2:00 or 3:00 in the morning, enjoying their freedom from your rules but damaging their memories, ability to focus, and internal clock. They nap when they shouldn't, mostly in class. (I can tell you from experience that a professor can see everyone who is sleeping, even in a huge lecture hall.) They are vulnerable to illness when you add those conditions to the close quarters of the petri dish known as a dormitory.

Mental health issues are more complicated—and more serious. Many mental health disorders, such as depression, become real (or manifest themselves) in late adolescence, when students are in their first years in college. I will discuss this at length in the Strategy #8 chapter, but it is worth repeating many times. Depression and other mental health challenges are serious, significant obstacles to college success. They can even be life-threatening. Other related issues, such as eating disorders and managing learning disabilities, also require sustained attention as impediments to academics and to their happiness.

So we can start this discussion of balance by saying, unequivocally, that you can and should continue to monitor, worry about, and act on any health challenges. What role you play academically is arguable (and I will argue about that), but you can be confident that you should and must be your son's or daughter's strongest partner and advocate for their health. Ask about what they are eating, how much they are sleeping, and what exercise they are getting.

If you know they are vulnerable to, or have experienced, mental health issues, do not hesitate to share this with the college, particularly if the issues are serious. Do not worry that the college will now doubt that your student should remain enrolled. American higher education takes pride in its commitment to every student's health and eventual graduation. Once they have admitted the student, there is no going back. So you are free to reach out to an academic advisor or the dean of students to express your concerns or to share a student's health history. That can be done in confidence, making sure that your student does not learn you have shared this. But the ethics and propriety of this is quite clear. College administrators cannot help a student if they do not know the challenges he or she faces.

Similarly, you need to reciprocate on these issues. Provided that a student has waived his or her right to confidentiality (itself a difficult issue), you may learn from the university of these mental health issues. Understandably, you will be upset and distressed, but you need to set aside any feelings of guilt or shame so that you can support any needed intervention. Struggling students need to know you support whatever therapy or medications are required. You may feel helpless from a distance, so you will have to trust the college and the student to cope with the problems. If they know you are behind them on this, you have done a great good.

You'll be relieved that I'm moving on to other topics.

Another area where you can be an old-style parent is to offer ongoing support for the hard work, difficult choices, and inevitable failures that your daughter or son will face. Everyone needs a cheerleader, someone who loves them, expresses approval, and offers encouragement when things have gone wrong. You're familiar with this job, and you should not doubt its ongoing and crucial importance. Facing a poor grade, a failed relationship, or a painful athletic loss is difficult enough without the disapproval of our parents. Empathize, sympathize, offer solace and warmth.

It will be tempting to judge and display your disappointment when things go wrong. Your feelings are real, but they are not helpful. You will continue to play a vital role in your son's or daughter's college life if you only do this. They need to know you care and that you worry about them, while you restrain yourself from criticism and judgments that do nothing more than allow you to vent.

How to Strike a New Balance

Helping them stay healthy and offering encouragement are easy choices. Do that. Giving them room so that they can become more independent and take ownership over their education is more difficult. To keep this discussion parallel to that of your student, I will paraphrase the advice I give them in *Dean's List* because it's important that the conversation about moving toward independence align. Our generation has created a new model for parenting, one steeped in open communication and mutual respect. So let's follow that model here as you consider five suggestions for the growth of your relationship:

1. *Imagine a different kind of relationship with your daughter or son.* It can be difficult to get somewhere without picturing what that will look like. You want to feel that it's the right place to go. So you should be sure you're comfortable with a vision in which you treat each other as adults who respect each other. What would life be like if things changed in that way? What advantages and disadvantages are there? You can accept the future or embrace it. If you embrace it, you're more likely to have a role in shaping what that looks like. So imagine that place and work to get there.

2. *Help them to become less needy.* As parents, we enable our children all the time. We do the dishes when they should. We make their beds instead of yelling at them for the fifth time. In college, they may turn to us often for advice, guidance, and approval. Don't

be cheap with the approval, but hand out guidance cautiously to avoid that kind of enabling. If you are more reluctant to solve the problem, your daughter or son will have to do that. If you respond to their question or request by first asking what they would like or need to do, that gives power back to them. Know your limits, too, and suggest that they ask other people: professors, deans, coaches, and friends. You may be the first among advisors, but you should repeatedly point out (a) there are other people to consult, and (b) they will have to sort out the advice themselves. Allow them to take prudent risks by showing your hesitation to solve problems that they can solve. It will send the signal that it's better to grow up than to be right.

3. *Encourage them to proactively explore their opportunities.* It may become clear that the plan you thought they were following is not working. Encourage them to build their own plan—with little or no input from you. Assure them that it's OK to have doubts and insecurities as they think about this. That it is natural and understandable to see an open and borderless landscape. Tell them that it takes hard work—self-assessment, counseling, research, experimentation, and experience—to build any plan, however tentative. Pushing them to do those things, thinking creatively and openly, will help. Reassuring them that you will support the outcome will be invaluable, though difficult for you. Again, a light touch with steady advice will keep you involved at an appropriate distance.

4. *Let them take a stand against you.* On the face of it, this might sound crazy. Encourage them to defy you? Quite the contradiction. And you may strongly feel that you are in the right (even though you may not be). So, why would it make sense to let them argue? Because that is part of the process of separation. Adolescents need a sense of power to feel good and strong. Standing up to you, as they did over a hundred things while living at home, is part of that process of maturing. So a showdown on whether to drop or keep Organic Chemistry may be one of those same moments. They say drop, you say, "Stick with it." Appreciate that you may be wrong and that they need moments like this to become confident and independent.

5. *Leave them alone.* If you can't think what to do, do nothing. Being

a good parent in a shifting environment has never been simple or easy. You already know that—doing your best under circumstances that have bedeviled humans in every era, in every place. If those circumstances stump you, just say you don't know or don't make that phone call at all. You may have built the habit of constant communication, aided by countless new technologies. But it's possible that distance and separate reflection can lead to calmer, more sustainable decisions than simply charging at each other over and over. Remember that the desired outcome is their success and happiness, and a little distance might be the path to follow to let that happen. Don't worry. It's just temporary.

Around the Kitchen Table

I'm guessing this has not been a fun read. I've pushed you to take stock of your relationship with your college student. I've insisted that you continue to worry about their health while taking the difficult steps of creating greater distance between you. Since more independence is inevitable, you might as well manage that more consciously. The glide path will be smoother for you, and more effective for them, if you approach it willingly.

Willingly does not have to be *happily*. You can and will have many doubts of the wisdom of giving them more space. You will see that some choices are not prudent and will end badly, or so you think. It's also likely that you'll be watching uncomfortably as they make poor choices. You will need to decide how poor they are, what impact they might have, and whether they were made based on ignorance or inexperience. You may agonize over this. *What do I do?*

At that moment, try for a lighter touch than usual. You can be supportive without commanding, ask questions without intruding, and offer gentle advice without dictating. Sure, urge them to go to the Career Center as a freshman. They will certainly benefit. But you can't force them to do that, even if they understand your reasoning. And sure, overstep sometimes. That's going to happen, as you will err on the side of protectiveness, especially around health issues.

Just know that all of this will change with time. Time is an independent student's greatest ally, as my neighbor pointed out. You'll become more accepting of a lesser role, perhaps relieved by it, as time passes and you see the benefits. You'll worry less often, and you'll ask better questions. More importantly, you'll see that the influence you will always have—the values, respect, curiosity, work ethic, priorities, dreams—are already baked into your child. You will always have a role to play, as you are a vital partner in this adventure. But as that role lessens, have faith that you have already done your job. And they are thriving because you did it well.

* Are you getting enough sleep?
* What are you eating?
* I'm worried you're not involved in enough activities, especially exercise and sports. Should I be?
* Let's talk about talking. Should I be calling you more or less often? Texting? Should I let you initiate those things?
* Do you need any help with anything? Do you know who can give you that help?
* How are you feeling generally? Confident, worried, happy, sad, connected, lost?
* Before you left, we talked about a plan for college. Was that a good idea?
* If you need a plan at all, do you understand that it belongs to you? What does that mean?

Understand Where They Are

I t's Friday night. Do you know where your daughter or son is?" This question may have bedeviled you throughout their high school experience. You wanted to know where they were going, with whom, and whether alcohol would be available. You insisted on updates if any of that changed and then waited for their texts all evening long. Of course, you were worried for their safety, but you also wanted to know more about their environment. You did the same for their schools, going to Back to School Nights, attending teacher conferences, and meeting with administrators and counselors as needed.

Now that they're in college, you have no idea what is happening and with whom. The college environment is completely unfamiliar if you did not attend a US college yourself. If you did, you are out of touch with today's college life, even if you attended the same institution. You may have to take it on faith that the college or university will support your son or daughter, which may be one reason you chose a more famous institution for them. That brand carries with it reassurance.

But, really, you don't have answers to the questions I pose to students in *Dean's List*: Who are the people on this campus, what do they do, how are they organized, what do they care about, and how do I fit in? The answers to these questions will affect their success in important ways, particularly in their relationships with faculty. You *know* where they are, but do you *understand* where they are?

Now, I've just made the case in the Strategy #2 chapter that you should allow them to become more independent from you. So how do you pose these questions, or act on their answers, without violating that principle? What follows, therefore, is meant to inform and reassure you about the institution you have trusted with your child. But it will also give you pointers on whether and when to connect to that college or university or how to counsel your son or daughter to make that connection. You do not need to be ignorant or helpless to give them the respect and freedom to handle their college life more independently.

And you'll feel a lot better, on a Friday night or any other, that you understand where they are and what it all means. And that is why Strategy #3 for supporting college success is *Understand Where They Are*.

The Most Important Players: The Faculty

Without doubt, the most important players on any campus, and therefore those who affect your child's life more than any other, are the faculty. They are responsible for her or his education, but they come to that task differently than high school teachers. Your expectations of how they do that, and your understanding of what other roles they play, can help you advise your student on how much to build this critical relationship.

Let's begin by noting that university faculty do not have the same training as their high school counterparts. High school faculty are teachers first and last. They have been trained to organize, lead, and assess students in developmentally appropriate ways, informed by the latest literature on effective teaching and learning. They have been taught how to run a classroom, manage its schedule, and handle many learning styles. Public schools require certification, meaning teachers have to be trained, often working as a student-teacher to practice their new craft.

In contrast, university or college faculty generally must be trained as researchers first, with little attention paid to their teaching skills. Most academic disciplines require a PhD, a doctorate in philosophy—a term dating from the Middle Ages to encompass most subject matter. Doctoral programs are designed to prepare their graduate students to be scholars, not teachers, by introducing them to the literature in their field and showing them how to conduct research. The literature is foundational, as your research must both respect and add to it in a significant, defensible manner.

Your daughter or son will belong to a college or school within a university, but a graduate student belongs to a single department, such as Mathematics, Political Science, or Electrical Engineering. They usually apply to that department directly, intent on working with the specific faculty and facilities there. They likely get their funding from that department, and their professional lives are in the hands of those faculty.

Graduate students generally need to take classes in preparation for comprehensive examinations and to complete a dissertation. They absorb the scholarly literature at a breakneck speed in those classes, and the exams verify that they have that literature at their command to navigate the research they will do to advance their careers. The dissertation might be a series of papers or a large single project meant to make a distinctive mark on their field. They will be hired into professorships at another college or university based primarily on this research.

It doesn't get any easier on them after that. To secure tenure, or a permanent position in the department, professors must continue contributing to their field with peer-reviewed books and articles. The more publications, the better, as they are a measure of their productivity, their ability to stand up to national and international scrutiny, and their contribution to raising the profile of the home department.

Wait. What about teaching? Like the rest of us, graduate students have to pay their bills. They often get a tuition waiver and a stipend to make this risky financial investment work, a stipend often earned by teaching. Graduate students serve as teaching and laboratory assistants to professors, helping them with managing breakout sections or meetings, and handling most or all of the grading of exams and papers. But they receive little or no training to do this teaching, learning on the job, often with inconsistent feedback on how to improve.

This arrangement begins the tentative partnership between research and teaching that will mark their careers. Scholars are trained to do research. It was what they want and must do to secure positions, tenure (more on this in a moment), and prestige. Their relationship with teaching is more complex. Most professors enjoy their teaching, but they don't get much credit for it professionally. They know they have to teach, but there are few resources to improve and not much attention if they do. Indeed, faculty who teach well and with passion do so despite expectations on them. All of this leaves them with a contradictory, confusing environment. And it leaves your daughter or son in an educational culture that is not as simple as the one they had in high school.

What You Can Do

American higher education is a complex culture and industry. As consumers of education, you and your son or daughter naturally expect that the purpose of this industry is to teach students. In fact, higher education is charged with discovery, research, patient care, and the management of libraries, laboratories, and a wide variety of properties, such as archaeological sites and nature preserves. Professors are involved in all of these enterprises, serving on university and discipline-based committees, organizing conferences, managing research teams, recruiting and mentoring doctoral students and other professors, and applying to foundations and the government for grant money.

The research enterprise alone would be a full-time job. There are data sets to compile and analyze, manuscripts to write and rewrite. Laboratory experiments might take years to yield important findings. Fieldwork at geological sites, in marine forests, and on ancient ruins can take them to every corner of the world. None of this work is guaranteed to succeed, either, as findings may be unimportant or negative. And their publication is subject to competitive review by demanding scholars. So a professor could work on a question for years, only to have her peers reject the importance of her findings.

You begin to see that teaching your child is on a very long list of things that university and college faculty do as professionals. To most promotion and tenure committees, and to future employers, teaching is a nice addition to a career marked by research contributions. This is even true in small colleges that have no graduate programs because their faculty were trained as researchers, remain committed to being published scholars, and need to maintain their reputation outside the classroom.

If you are not familiar with American higher education, these few pages on the life of a faculty member might be difficult to accept. *I am paying tuition so these guys can publish in academic journals!* You might be upset, even outraged, that teaching is a lower priority, particularly as poor or indifferent instruction might hurt your own son or daughter.

So what do you do? How can you support your student in this environment? I have several suggestions:

1. *Appreciate that active research informs good teaching.* Faculty, deans, and college presidents have made this argument for years. And there is merit to it. To stay current and competitive, active researchers stay on top of the literature so their teaching reflects the latest findings. A researcher brings the passion of new discovery to a classroom, as well, making the real-time case that knowledge is a moving target, not set and ready to be taught. More broadly, understanding and appreciating a professor's many duties will help your student to respect the real person.

2. *Be sure your son or daughter has realistic expectations.* You are both consumers. So you should know what you're buying. You're not paying for showmanship or entertainment from an instructor but a journey of engaged, skeptical discovery. That means your standard for teaching may be misaligned. When you evaluate college teaching by its own standards, you will find plenty of variation. Some scholars are great, dedicated teachers. Others are not. But it makes no sense to put either group on a scale that doesn't fit.

3. *Encourage your student to join the faculty's world.* Once he or she has realized that the teaching environment is different than they expected, and different from the high school tradition (itself imperfect, let me remind you), they can think about joining the culture of research and discovery. Undergraduate research has become an important part of university and college life, offering students their own chance to add to knowledge, even to publish findings. I coached hundreds of such projects as a professor on the faculty of the University of California, Los Angeles. My students gained a strong sense of ownership that made them feel powerful.

4. *Tell them that they need to shop around.* Again, think of yourselves as consumers. Just because all faculty are researchers does not mean they are all poor teachers. Indeed, most faculty are dedi-

cated teachers despite the lack of importance to their careers. But because they vary in skill and enthusiasm, your daughter or son should look around. Use the shopping period in the early days of a semester to compare multiple choices. Consider taking smaller courses or those offered by less-well-known departments. At Johns Hopkins University, one of our best instructors taught Portuguese—not a language many students chose to study. Your student should take advantage of any course evaluation publication or Web site, though they should balance that feedback knowing student tastes vary, too.

5. *Remind them that all professors have office hours.* I will touch on this point again, but it's a point worth repeating. College professors can seem intimidating, despite our best efforts to be approachable and friendly. (Of course, there are those that are neither!) So it is not surprising that students often fail to ask questions in class, hesitate before they dispute a professor's argument, and resist meeting them during office hours. Yet all these choices are mistakes. Professors want and expect to be engaged, challenged, and questioned. It's disappointing when students do not. Encourage your son or daughter to be brave. Tell them to visit office hours, ready with some specific questions from the notes or readings, and discover that they will be both welcomed and enlightened.

6. *Do not contact them yourself.* The first error that concerned parents make is to contact faculty members directly. You may have noticed that, as your child progressed through school, his or her teachers became more and more inaccessible. But even high school teachers welcomed your e-mail, call, or appointment—if only to address problems before the administration became annoying and involved. At the college level, this is just not done. College professors insist that their relationship is with their students, not with you. There are legal restrictions from FERPA (Family Educational Rights and Privacy Act of 1974), the US federal law protecting a student's privacy, and there are cultural expectations that parents and families remain in the background. So, please, do not contact them directly. That's your son's or daughter's job.

More Players

A college campus is filled with professionals, important players to your son's or daughter's success. You might be surprised that the president is not among them. Most parents look to college or university presidents as the most powerful people on campus. And maybe they are. They are certainly the most visible and famous. It's tempting to think of them as administrators, leaders, or managers. If they were, they could be very useful to your family. But they aren't. They are strategists, setting the direction of the university with the support of the board of trustees and fund-raisers.

You may know that collecting tuition is never enough for a college or university to survive financially. These institutions need many sources of revenue, including research grants, endowment income, and annual gift campaigns. A crucial piece to this mission is collecting major gifts from important donors, often alumni of the college. Those donors expect to build a relationship with the college's chief officer, the president, and they will not be writing a big check unless asked by the president in person. So the president may appear to have administrative powers to make your life easier, when she or he is actually spending most of their time raising money.

So who can help you and your daughter or son? The cast of characters is long, so let me highlight a few. The general rule that parents should not make direct contact applies here as it does to faculty. Under most conditions, you need to let your son or daughter contact these people. He or she needs to build the confidence to handle the problem, and that is the expectation of these individuals.

There are exceptions, of course. As I discussed in Strategy #2 on your changing relationship, if your child has significant health issues, if they are in danger, if there are seismic changes at home, then you should feel free to reach out, specifically to a dean. At that moment, culture and tradition make no sense. Do what you need to do.

For normal problems, direct your student to one of these people:

- *Resident assistants, or RAs.* Colleges with residential programs and dormitories will hire other students as the first point of contact. RAs live in the dorms, usually down the hall, charged with providing advice, mediation between bickering roommates, supervision of policies (such as prohibitions on drinking), and other services. They are a good starting point if your daughter or son is not sure where to go next with a problem. Just understand that RAs are students themselves so they lack perspective, experience, and authority.

- *Teaching assistants, or TAs.* I have mentioned that faculty often begin their teaching career by serving as teaching assistants when they were in graduate school. Colleges with no graduate programs draw TAs from talented, successful upper-class students. TAs are invaluable to students who need help with an assignment, a paper, or an exam preparation. As TAs often grade those requirements, it makes sense to know what they know. They usually run sections, or breakout sessions, to support larger lecture courses. Sections are usually optional, but students should go to all of them. Never turn down help. Like RAs, TAs have their limitations, but they are a great resource.

- *Directors.* Depending on the campus and its titling, directors are the most important hands-on administrators. They direct key support offices, such as disability services, tutoring, writer centers, academic advising, Greek life (for fraternities and sororities), community outreach, dining services, and residential life. These are go-to people who usually have the authority and certainly the skills to handle almost any problem that your student will encounter. Every college's Web site will list them with contact information, often under "Who We Are" on an office's site. Best for your student to make an appointment, but better to drop in than not get help.

- *Deans.* Again, institutions vary in how they title and organize the administrative staff, but colleges have a long tradition of naming top administrators as deans. A large university usually divides itself into schools, such as Arts and Sciences or Engineering. The dean of that school is its academic and administrative leader. But "dean" can also apply to those leading academic offices, such as Advising or Undergraduate Education, as well as those in student life. At Johns Hopkins University, our Dean of Students was responsible for dozens of offices that affected student life, from athletics to academic integrity. She always said if parents didn't know whom to ask, she was the one who could direct them.

- *Provosts.* It is very unlikely that you will have to deal with a university or college provost. As the chief academic officer responsible for the faculty and the teaching/research enterprise, the provost is considered the number two leader to the president. They are important because the health, success, and strength of the faculty is the foundation for any college. A student might never encounter the provost, but it can be useful to know that faculty nominally report to the provost. I say nominally because faculty are independent, often armed with permanent tenure, so a provost has limited tools to make changes or hold them accountable.

Around the Kitchen Table

When I would welcome parents to events at Johns Hopkins University, I always started by thanking them for entrusting my colleagues and me with their children. It is a great honor and responsibility to be given, year after year, a new group of freshmen or first-year students, nervous, eager, and full of high expectations.

I have found that these expectations, particularly of faculty, are not just high but misplaced or poorly informed. They call their instructors "teachers," not professors, expecting that they can continue to learn as they did in high school. Yet college faculty do not see themselves that way, if only because they have too many other jobs: researcher, grant writer, graduate student recruiter, conference organizer, and on and on. More importantly, college professors think of themselves as partners with students on a journey of mutual discovery and insight. Knowledge is not handed down by teacher to pupil. It is revealed by hard work and research debated, considered, and shared.

If you and your student are to take full advantage of the tuition you are paying, if you are looking to maximize your return on investment for the greatest payoff, you should know what you're buying. This chapter, I hope, has helped you understand more fully the life of a faculty member, in particular, so that you appreciate your investment and know how to best navigate it.

It might also help, as you start conversations with questions like those below, that American colleges and universities pioneered the principle that they should educate and nurture the whole student.

American faculty are productive scholars, to be sure, but they are also engaged teachers—provided you know what they are teaching. And they are supported and surrounded by an army of administrators who take a comprehensive approach to college life. These administrators take a personal and serious stake in the success of your son or daughter. Your student is in good hands, but it helps to know whose hands.

* Tell me about your professors. What are they researching? What is their specialty?
* What kind of teaching styles are your professors showing? Is that different than you expected? How do you have to adapt to those styles?
* Have you gone to your professors' office hours? I'm sure that's intimidating, but it's important to understand them better and to get help.
* What do you know about your TA? Have you asked her or him questions about the course? Have you been going to the sections? I know they're optional.
* Have you thought about doing any research with one of your professors?
* Do you know where to go to get help? Like the writing center or tutoring?
* Colleges don't really like it when parents contact them. Do you understand what that means for you? If I'm not contacting them, how can I help?

Appreciate Their Academic Choices

My family has a favorite Vietnamese restaurant, a pho eatery called, well, Pho Eatery. Pho is a traditional noodle soup in Vietnam, usually a spicy beef broth with rice noodles and meat shavings into which you can toss bean sprouts, basil leaves, lime juice, and Sriracha sauce. I always get the P3 from the menu—beef broth with brisket and flank.

I could choose any one of dozens of offerings. I could get the pho with any other combination with tripe, soft tendon, or steak. I know what steak is. But I'm not sure I've ever had tripe, despite traveling to nearly 50 countries and living in both Europe and South Asia. "Soft tendon" sounds kind of disgusting, even though that reaction, I'm sure, is culturally biased. Why is it soft?

So I'm safe with P3. I know what that looks and tastes like. Getting either brisket or flank seemed too safe and dull, but getting both creates the illusion that I know what I'm talking about. In fact, I really know nothing about Vietnamese cooking, and I hesitate to be more adventurous.

Now, consider how this dynamic of choosing what is safe and known affects your family as you discuss what your daughter or son might study in college. They will be looking at a long menu of courses, which may number in the hundreds, drawn from dozens of departments—even at small colleges. Large universities may offer thousands of courses, representing the power and breadth of their faculty that populate many schools: Public Health, Arts and Sciences, Agriculture, Law, Medicine, and many others. Course catalogues, once printed and now online, are extraordinary documents, covering a vast intellectual landscape from anthropology to zoology.

But a vast course catalogue is also complex, confusing, and intimidating. Like a long menu in an unfamiliar or foreign restaurant, it offers many choices but no easy way to navigate them. Your son or daughter may be tempted to look for the familiar, those offerings like P3. They'll shy from "soft tendons," courses that look difficult or strange.

And you are likely to enable or even require that they think this way. Your own inexperience with any or all university disciplines might make you pressure them, consciously or not, to make safer, better-known choices. Political science, not sociology. Biology, not earth sciences. Economics, not sociology. You'll start rationalizing this quickly, thinking the ones you know will lead to lucrative careers, when you may have no basis for connecting those two points in time.

There is another, more compelling and immediate problem. For a student to succeed in college, they must make academic and coursework choices that fit their skills, needs, and talents. It requires that they have the freedom to explore widely enough to find that fit. Your son or daughter will need your encouragement, blessing, and advice to start and keep to that search until they find a home. There are many factors to success, and your familiarity with a discipline or course topic is not on that list. For you to support their success, then, you will need to be open-minded and supportive of exploration. In other words, you will need to embrace Strategy #4 for supporting college success, *Appreciate Their Academic Choices*.

The Link between Exploration and Success

It is likely that your son or daughter has heard the message from their college that they should take full advantage of the wide academic choices available to them. The college has a lot of good reasons to do that. They can't afford to have students congregate in just a few areas of study, leaving faculty in other departments unoccupied. That's wasteful. They are bothered when talented faculty who would love more students go unappreciated. That's hurtful. And they are offended that students do not value all disciplines equally. That's unthinking.

I have a different, immediate reason to urge your student to explore widely and for you to actively support them: academic success. Faculty want their students to do well, of course, but your family has a more personal stake in this. College students need to own their education, to feel connected to their studies in deeply personal ways. For them to do the hard work needed for success, they need to find strong motivation from within, tapping into their own curiosity and desire to learn.

They will not tap into that motivation without finding topics, ideas, methods, and ultimately disciplines that excite them. If particle physics holds no interest for a student, it will take great external force—likely coming from you—to push them to learn it well enough to excel. And you are neither there to give that push nor should you want to if you're hoping they will grow to independent adulthood.

Indeed, if the course of study offers little pleasure intellectually, they will be consumed with resentment and even anger. "This is so boring," their brains will cry out each time they pick up a textbook, review notes for an exam, or decide on a paper topic. Anger will create a negative loop that will consume them, their studies, and their relationship with you, if you're the one responsible for their choices.

It is crucial, therefore, that you help them to find a set of courses that fits them well. You can play an important and positive role in this enterprise, encouraging them to experiment and explore. Beyond offering the basics of support and love, you can say, "Give it a try. You might like it." Or, "If you really hate that course, maybe you should find another direction." The rewards will be many, as they take responsibility for their choices and enjoy the challenges ahead, without the burden of resentment.

Four Questions to Ask Them

It will help in offering this encouragement if you consider asking them four important questions:

1. What do you want to learn?
2. What does the college require you to do?

3. What skills do you want to build?
4. Where is the surprise?

What Do You Want to Learn?

As I mentioned in Strategy #1, I've always been surprised that this is not the first question on every college student's list. It seems pretty simple. You're going to college to learn, so what do you want to learn? This is a healthy question to ask your son or daughter because you're challenging them to think more selectively about their choices, to consider how they will own their education, and to be more mindful of their natural curiosity. If high school was an intellectual appetizer, what more do they want to taste or try? They haven't gone to school only to check boxes and fill requirements but to build a wider perspective, to ask interesting questions, and to wonder why.

Asking what to learn does not have to be connected to an academic or a professional plan. Why not learn more about insect life or the behavior of wolves? How were Native Americans affected by smallpox, and how does that differ from the effects of other epidemics in less developed nations? What is anti-matter? How do Arthurian legends explain early political development in England? What are the reasons why people get depressed? How have communications technologies affected pop culture? Questions like these have inherent value. To be educated, or learned, one should ask such questions and find their answers. To be curious is to be human.

Still, if you must see utility in asking, "What do you want to learn?" play a more pointed role in seeing what fields truly interest them. Pre-medical students must complete a list of coursework before applying, but there are many ways to do that. Any biology course, from cellular to ethology, would do—so why not take one that satisfies their curiosity. There are several approaches to physics. Math requirements can be fulfilled with statistics. And the need for an English course is wide open, covering the literature of any culture or time period. Which one is more interesting?

When you start asking questions about specific subjects to learn, you underscore the importance of curiosity, and you push them to be aware of questions that come naturally to them. American colleges give you the freedom to take different paths to the same destination, whether toward a particular major (most offer many choices within that program) or to a career (more on that in Strategy #9). So encouraging them to ask themselves what they find interesting will support their quest to find an exciting, self-motivated path that will feed their curiosity and help them succeed academically.

What Are the Requirements?

One challenge of living apart from your son's or daughter's campus is that you likely have very little sense of what they *have* to do. A college's general education, or distribution, requirements should have been something your student considered when they chose a college to attend. Is a college open or restrictive about registering for coursework outside the major? Are there specific core courses they must all take? Do they need to distribute their courses in special ways (e.g., two courses in each of five areas, such as the humanities, social sciences, and laboratory sciences)?

Applicants rarely think this far ahead when they look at colleges, but these rules do affect how much freedom they will have. And that will affect how much they feel some courses need to be gotten out of the way. That attitude turns a course, which is an invitation to learn and explore, into a chore for some students. On the other hand, many students lack the experience or maturity to navigate a wide-open landscape with no markers or requirements. They would just wander around unproductively, not building on any lessons nor creating frameworks to learn more effectively. That may be taking a liberal education too far.

But it is smart and healthy to ask your daughter or son what the college asks them to do. Those requirements, with the help of a good academic advisor, can be managed over time. They rarely have to be done quickly, but they do have to be completed by graduation. You won't want them stuck in a summer class, filling a last-minute requirement.

What Skills Do You Need?

This question can provoke interesting conversations about the purpose of a college education. If you have experienced an American college education yourself, you'll know that expertise, or deep knowledge of a subject or discipline, is not an expected outcome. Higher education has many goals, from creating a sense of global citizenship to an appreciation of other cultures. Transforming students into experts is not among them. That is reserved for graduate school.

But you can ask what kinds of skills they might want to acquire, skills that could enable them to thrive in a variety of professional settings. Communications tops that list. Can they write really well, crafting clear, jargon-free, accessible, and argumentative prose? Taking writing-intensive courses is a must, particularly for those who are avoiding them for lack of confidence with this vital, professional skill.

The ability to speak effectively is crucial in most professional settings. But if they are taking only large lecture classes and labs, they will not have the chance to speak up and practice how to present themselves orally. If you point this out, they may be more likely to take smaller classes or seminars. And the subject doesn't matter, provided that they have the chance to talk.

A global economy requires foreign language skills. Whether building on a high school language curriculum or branching out to new languages (Italian? German? Swahili? Arabic? Mandarin? Portuguese?), finding the slot to plug in a language can be an important investment. Want to work in international finance? German or Japanese could be a skill that distinguishes one resumé from thousands.

Other skills include the ability to use statistics, write programs, construct Web sites, analyze budgets and finances, conduct chemical experiments, and interview subjects. Again, these skills do not require specific courses, for the most part. So, by asking what skills they would like to build, you are not restricting their substantive choices as much as underscoring the need to know what they're getting with a college education.

Where Is the Surprise?

Much of life is serendipity. How do you make friends and fall in love? Mostly by accident, catching someone's attention or falling into conversation. Meeting someone requires being in the same place at the same time, and both of those have too many variables to predict. So it can be with finding interesting courses, subjects, majors, and even degrees. We can only do so much planning, and the rest we have to leave to fate. One of the unexpected pleasures of required courses is that, if students are paying attention and have set aside resentment, they will discover unexpectedly interesting topics. I have known many students who took a course in sociology or anthropology to fulfill a requirement, only to be swept up in the subject matter. And that can lead to a course of study powered by curiosity—a recipe for academic success.

You can play an important role in encouraging the kind of experimentation that results in unexpected and successful discoveries. While talking about required courses, for example, press them on what was surprising, fun, or provocative. Explore how strongly they feel, or push them to give you examples of what was especially interesting. Ask them whether they want to pursue it further. If they cannot give examples, then challenge them to find courses that will offer those surprises.

If there is an open slot in a heavy schedule, encourage them to try different courses. History of Art? Musicology? Archaeology? Comparative Religions? If there is a January or intersession period in their academic year, urge them to take advantage. At Johns Hopkins University, intersession offered dozens of low-credit, low-pressure courses on many fun and provocative subjects. Their college or university offers these courses for this very reason. You're paying for it. They should take advantage and look for the surprise within.

Around the Kitchen Table

Parenting a successful high school student may have required a lot of pushing. You may have been a taskmaster, reminding your daughter or son of upcoming assignments, demanding that they turn off their phones and get to work, and expecting them to go to every class and listen respectfully to the teacher. Maybe you had to tell them when to go to sleep, after telling them for the hundredth time to put away their clothes and tidy their room.

Here, for college life, you can play an important role in pushing them to explore, to take full advantage of the curricular treasures that even the smallest college will offer. Be mindful that neither of you likely know the full range of available disciplines, unfamiliar with their content, methods, or driving questions. If you can admit to that ignorance, you can point out to your daughter or son that simply because they do not know a subject does not mean it doesn't hold great promise as a place to thrive.

Even if I can't get you to see that grades should have less importance, know that students will get better grades if they are studying subjects they love. And they won't find those subjects without experimenting and exploring—a task that you can support.

And you can support that by asking questions like those posed throughout this chapter. Try to reserve your judgment, staying modest in your ability to assess their value or outcome: "Earth Science? What is that?" Resist the temptation to dismiss what you don't know. Showing intellectual modesty and open-mindedness will be a powerful model for your daughter or son. "If Mom and Dad are asking me to explore, then I guess it's OK. They just want me to find a home in a big place." And they won't find that home without trying something other than the P3.

➡ * Are you having fun with your coursework? What do I mean by "fun"?

 * What do you know about the university's requirements? What's your approach to them?

 * When you were in high school, what were the subjects you loved most? Can you figure out what they have in common?

 * Think about trips we've taken or activities you've done that have provoked good questions. Are those worth asking through your coursework?

* It's a good idea to walk away from college with key skills. What do you think those could be, and how would you get or build them?
* Does your college have ways to sample new subject areas, such as an intersession? Have you considered doing that and trying something new?
* Have you been to any of the lectures or guest speakers offered on campus? That is worth your time, if only to find something new.

Disconnect Majors and Careers

As a parent separated from the college experience, you may have difficulty seeing the joys and advantages of focusing on the intellectual experience, on setting educational goals based on what to learn and what skills to develop. You can't see what is happening in the classroom and in conversations outside it. You're not living the challenges of studying, nor appreciating the lively campus environment. Because you can't see the process of learning, you may default to looking at outcomes.

In Strategy #1, I suggested that paying too much attention to grades as an outcome is misleading and problematic. When students focus on grades, they fail to appreciate how far they have come, and they become obsessed with pleasing instructors rather than taking advantage of the fuller learning experience.

Another outcome that attracts the attention of parents is what major a student chooses. Majors (or concentrations in some colleges) are the most obvious product of a college education. I can say, for example, "I went to Yale and majored in history." There. In eight words, I have summarized my college credentials. I even could say that I earned a degree in history at Yale. Now you might think that all I did at Yale was study history.

If you think that way about everyone in college, you will conclude that the principal credential of an American college education is the major. And you would draw the easy conclusion that such a credential is a prerequisite to a clear career path.

But you would be wrong on both counts. Students do not really earn a degree in one discipline. Rather, they earn a major as part of a wider liberal arts experience. And what they choose as a major has poor predictive power over career outcomes. It might be reassuring to think otherwise, but that's not how American colleges work. This reflects a wider ambivalence in higher education about the importance of expertise. On the one hand, colleges believe that a wider education is important to developing a fully functioning, global citizen. On the other hand, faculty believe that focus on a discipline promotes rigor. A major, therefore, is a compromise between those positions.

That is why to support your student so she or he might take full advantage of college you need to know Strategy #5, *Disconnect Majors and Careers*. And you need to make peace with the notion that your student's choice of a major is not going to answer the question, What will they do after they graduate? You want that reassurance. Maybe you crave it, if only to prove that four years of tuition is a worthwhile investment. But their major is not going to deliver that clarity for you.

Majors ≠ Careers

The evidence of the disconnect between majors and careers can be found in the alumni community of your son's or daughter's college or university. Students can research this themselves, asking the simple question, What do the alumni do? The answer will be hundreds of professions, following thousands of unique career paths. And then you can ask your student whether majors were a good predictor of those outcomes.

They can do this in two directions. First, they could take a list of majors and track what happened to those alumni in a given major. What are history majors like me doing now? When I was at Yale, history was the most popular major, and my fellow "historians" split into dozens of professions: lawyers, doctors, business executives, chefs, politicians, management consultants and more. Sure, there are some patterns to be found. Science and math majors leaned more toward scientific or medical careers. Engineers often became engineers. But these were the exceptions, and the power of the major usually weakened quickly as other experiences and training took hold.

Second, your daughter or son could look at those alumni in a specific profession and look backward in time to see what majors they chose. Again, they will find no easy connection, causal or otherwise. Look at doctors. Think they all majored in biology? Think again. Medical schools have little interest in building classes with uni-dimensional interests. That does not serve their faculty well, nor the patient community once they are trained. While biology would be a common choice for future doctors, dozens of other majors—English, political science, anthropology, Latin American studies—would be represented there, too.

Why the Disconnect?

As you continue this conversation with your son or daughter over the meaning and impact of a major, push them to consider why the connection between majors and careers would be so weak. If they can understand the weakness of this connection, the pressure on them to choose a perfect or professionally sensible major will lessen. Then they can elect a course of study that will be more enjoyable and lead to academic success.

So why the disconnect? There are many reasons. I've eluded to the first, the ambivalence of American higher education toward expertise, particularly at the undergraduate level. Others are related. A liberal arts major, with few exceptions (notably in engineering), is not a scholarly or pre-professional enterprise. A major is typically one-third of a full course of study. It may be constructed carefully, but it still represents a grouping of courses that likely do not build on one another nor hold together seamlessly. You can't expect your daughter or son to become expert or ready for a specific job with that training.

The randomness of coursework is compounded by the varying expertise of faculty. As most American faculty come from American colleges, you can expect that they have enjoyed a similarly eclectic education. Even their graduate programs allow for wide intellectual freedom, and they can decide what area or areas of research they want to pursue. Not surprisingly, the resulting mix of backgrounds creates an assortment of courses and requirements unique to a particular college. In other words, a political science major in one university is quite different from the same major in another.

As I will discuss further in Strategy #10, many other variables affect career choices and outcomes: where you live, whom you meet, experiences you have (or don't), natural and learned skills, and your work colleagues and bosses. Talk to your son or daughter about your own choices and history. How did your own career evolve? What affected your choices? Have you shifted careers, and, if so, what new variables presented the new opportunity? What specific experiences or people made you walk away from something? What attracted you to something else? How much freedom did you have to choose, and what affected that latitude?

You are a partner in your student's success, as I have argued before. And this is a critical conversation to have, one where your experience and professional perspective can be important. Your story is likely filled with many people and experiences you never anticipated, leading to career choices you never planned. If you received an undergraduate degree, especially in the United States, you probably followed a path affected by many more important factors than your major. Why would your son's or daughter's experience be different?

They need to hear this lesson, informed by your experience. And you need to be self-aware that your unpredictable path gives your student permission to experience their own path without the pressure of predicting all that will happen. Relieved of that pressure, they can enjoy the experience rather than fear the consequences of the choice.

Choose Wisely

If that conversation went well, your son or daughter might be less worried. But that doesn't make their choices easy—just less scary. Choosing a major may not write your professional future, but it is still important. Finding a great fit with their major course of study will affect how positively they feel about themselves, especially their sense of efficacy and competence. A good fit will mean coursework they enjoy, professors they will happily engage, and assignments that are challenges not burdens. All of that will result in a richer learning experience (and better grades).

So continue the conversation by asking questions I have drawn from *Dean's List*. If they are freed to choose a major on factors other than career implications, then they can

- *Be themselves.* They can create their own intellectual journey.
- *Love their choice.* If their major doesn't have to be "practical," then they can love it for its own merits.
- *Appreciate the value of their education.* No matter the major, they will get their (or your) money's worth.
- *Not be so hard on themselves.* If their choice doesn't affect them forever, then a poor choice won't handicap them.

Be Themselves

Parents tend to see a major as the most important credential from college, a key outcome of students' education, though I have argued this can be misleading. What they may not see is how important majors can be to a student's identity. As a parent, you are not seeing their social interactions, of course, so you likely don't appreciate that students find themselves boxed in by the reputations of their chosen majors. They feel the social pressures and expectations swirling around these choices, as some are admired (say, biomedical engineering) and others mocked as impractical (e.g., philosophy).

Understand that these dynamics can discourage them from making their best choices, from picking a major that suits their intellectual interests and skills really well. You may be feeding that dynamic consciously or not. You need to be mindful of these identity issues, as no one wants to be limited or dismissed by choices he or she has made.

Indeed, encouraging your students to be proud and unapologetic of their choices is a healthy way to reverse this thinking. If it helps, suggest that they answer the "What's your major?" question with a richer answer about their substantive interests. Explaining to their friends why they are considering or have chosen a major will help them learn to articulate their interests more effectively and help them stand up for strong, tailored choices.

Love Their Choice

Be careful how practical you label one major over another. Majors in the humanities are often labeled outdated, impractical, or too intellectual. Why would anyone wanting a job studying religious history or Japanese literature or English poetry? But you could ask the same question of majors that sound more practical. Economics is the study of self-interested behavior. It's not a course in business management. Political scientists like me generally know nothing about public policy. Physics may be a hard, fundamental science, but how useful is quantum theory on a daily basis?

These questions are really beside the point. Few, if any, majors available at most American colleges and universities are practical. In fact, majors are designed to open the world, deepen understanding, explore new ideas with depth, create and hone skills like conducting research, and enrich life. As a parent, you need to see the positive advantages of any major, rather than debating the practical merits. This is difficult to do, I know, given the uncertainties of life after college. There are better ways to prepare for that, as I'll outline in Strategy #10.

What deserves your support and focus is whether your son or daughter loves what they are studying. This is a simpler, more immediate question. If you keep repeating it, they will see that you care most about what they can handle now—the need to find a course of study that captures their imagination and inspires them to work hard. What classes do you love most? Why? Why not? These questions push them to dig more deeply into what types of academic experiences they enjoy, what learning styles fit them best, and what questions they take the most pleasure in answering.

Focusing on the love of learning will have a lasting impact, too. Your daughter or son needs to love the act of learning if they are to continue to enjoy success beyond college. Learning, and the hard work of studying, must bring them pleasure if they are to do it for the rest of their lives—a critical strategy to continuing professional success. If keeping up in their field or adapting to a new one is just a burden, handicapped by obligation, they won't do it or not do it well. But if you teach them to find and choose what they love to learn, that will give them the freedom to continue that habit for years to come.

Appreciate Their Education

Separating the choice of major from career decisions has another advantage. If your student puts the challenges of career navigation in another (albeit important) box, they can focus on the present and its challenges and rewards. Students already put off career questions, avoiding career centers at all costs. Those questions are big, scary, and probably unanswerable with any certainty. (Again, we'll tackle this in Strategy #10.) If you can support the choice of majors with the shorter-term goal of enjoying their studies and doing well in them, you will dampen the worries about career outcomes and help them see the importance of staying in the moment.

Staying in the moment will keep their priorities set on becoming a more learned person, as I suggest in Strategy #1. This will keep important values connected, such as the need to nurture curiosity, to grow in maturity and intellect, and to become a fully functioning global citizen. It will help you and your student be mindful of the education you are paying for, rather than hoping for guarantees about an uncertain professional future.

Forgive a Poor Choice

A final advantage to disentangling major choices from career options is that your daughter or son won't worry so much about making the wrong choice. This guidebook and *Dean's List*, you will find as you read Strategies #8 and #9, spend time considering failure. I want every student to succeed, of course, but I know the reality is that many do not. For a variety of reasons, they make poor choices. Sometimes, they made those choices with you or to please you. However independent they are, they can make decisions that put them in harm's way, experiencing coursework that is too difficult or uninteresting, with faculty who are not helpful or disconnected.

And they can choose the wrong major. They might do this because of pressure or reputation. They might have been good at a subject like chemistry in high school, but college-level studies turn out to be very different and disappointing. Things can go wrong along the way—introductory classes were appealing but upper-level requirements prove unexciting or unsuccessful. At Johns Hopkins University, I knew many students whose interests cooled over time or they encountered a really difficult required course. It happens, and you cope or change direction, depending on the severity.

These challenges are difficult enough to carry without worrying that career options have been cut off or destroyed. Tying a major to a career puts expectations on a major that failure cannot tolerate. If you had to major in biology to enjoy career success, and then biology is a bust, where are you? You can suffer through biology, taking courses you hate and earning grades that damage your transcript and future prospects— a seriously shortsighted approach that parents should not support—or choose an "impractical" major that condemns you to professional failure. This is a no-win situation, created by the thought that a particular major is a requirement for a happy career.

Do not enable this kind of thinking. Allow your son or daughter the freedom to choose coursework and majors in which they will succeed. Do not force them to be practical or career-savvy based on your impression of what fits those criteria. With freedom and lowered expectations of a major's purpose, they can choose as best they can. And if that choice turns out to be a mistake, they know they can recover, find a new course, and keep their career options open and strong.

Around the Kitchen Table

You're worried about your child's future. I get it. I empathize because I have a son in college, too. So you want your son or daughter to make good, practical choices that will lead to a safe, secure, and financially viable life. We love our children, and we want what is best for them. I completely agree, and I understand why picking a major would seem to be among the most important choices to ensure that future. I worry about what my son will pick as a major, too.

You'll have to admit, on reflection, that that's a lot of pressure for one choice. They better get it right, or the whole thing is ruined, right? Does that make sense? Does that fit with your (new) understanding of how American colleges teach or the educational meaning of a major? Does it even square with your own experience, if you attended a US college?

No, it doesn't.

Major courses of study do a lousy job of predicting the many career choices that graduates of American colleges and universities. I'm not saying they have no effect. I should also note they can be important prerequisites to graduate study in those areas. (Though I have a doctorate in political science and yet majored in history.) But there are too many other variables at work. You can safely believe that a successful college experience—as measured by intellectual depth, refined skills, sophisticated perspective, personal confidence, and the good grades that result from coursework chosen to satisfy curiosity not obligation—is enormously helpful, irrespective of major.

I would ask that, if you follow this logic, even to a few degrees off of your current position, you will help your son or daughter greatly. You will relieve the pressure of making the right, practical choice. You will signal that they should focus on learning and the academic process, as the outcomes will take care of themselves if they do. And you will relieve them of the burden that poor choices will cripple them and limit their choices.

Then their majors become an invitation to learning, and that should be your shared goal of a successful college education.

➡ * What are your college friends saying about picking majors? What are they thinking when considering their options? Does that make sense to you?
   * What are you hearing about whether some majors are better or more practical than others? What are the arguments against those attitudes?
   * What does "major" mean to you? What do you think the college means by that?
   * About how much of your classwork will be in your major? So what is important overall, your major or the other classwork?
   * What effect do you think your major will have on your career? What other things will be important?
   * (If applicable) Let me tell the story about how I chose my major and what effect it had on my professional choices. Try to listen and not roll your eyes.

* So what are you considering for majors? Compare them for me. What is interesting about them? What are the downsides to each of them?

Support How They Work

As my son progressed through high school, I started losing track of how he studied for his courses. He was disciplined about going to bed between 10 and 11 pm, which was a rare talent among his friends, but he did most of his studying in his room. And I really had no idea how he did his work. I only saw the outcomes: his attitude, his confidence, and his grades. His studying habits were a black box. I knew what went in, what came out, but little clue on how that transformation took place.

I could set parameters, however, and could drop in whenever I wanted. I could see that Netflix was too often playing on the laptop next to him. I could see when he looked disorganized. I knew when he was overly stressed. I also had every right to see his grades, talk to his teachers, and complain to the principal. If I thought he was staying up too late, I could insist he go to sleep. So his studies may have been a black box, but at least the black box was in my house.

Now that he is in college, I have no view of how he spends his day at all. He tells us, in the vaguest terms, of his course schedule. And we know he has rehearsals for his singing group and practices for his rock climbing and Ultimate Frisbee teams. As his time spreads out before him, I have no role to play, no supervision I can give. I can't tell him to go to sleep, and I certainly can't know if his study habits are sound, sensible, and successful. The black box just got bigger and is hours away from home.

For a lot of parents, this is a real test of trust and confidence in their son or daughter. You feel you can only hope that they have developed habits they will naturally use in college. You can believe that they appreciate the gravity of using those habits conscientiously because the stakes are high—for their immediate success, for their happiness and self-confidence, and for their career prospects. While it may matter less *what* they study, as I have argued in previous strategies, *how* they study is inarguably important.

To make this more stressful, the habits they developed in high school will be inadequate to the challenge of college. There are enough shifts in the structure, content, and intent in a university education that students must adapt or face significant challenges. It will not be enough, for example, to memorize formulas, historical dates, and Spanish vocabulary. Professors will demand higher levels of understanding, and the application of basic concepts or facts to much more complex situations and problems. They will need to grow and adjust how they study, as the definition of *studying* changes.

And you won't be able to see any of this.

So what can you do beyond hoping for the best? That is the purpose of this chapter, Strategy #6, *Support How They Work*. The basic message in this strategy is that study habits are a different matter than the decisions about courses and majors. While I have advised you to keep your distance on decision-making, I find merit and wisdom in asking them what they are doing and how they are studying.

It will help them to hear your reassurance that, though the ground is shifting under them, you have confidence they will make adjustments. And they are more likely to make those adjustments if you are aware of what is needed, particularly if you talk about this in their first weeks on campus.

Strategic Study Skills

Let's start by exploring the concept of the *strategic student*—a new role they will need to play, an adjustment they will need to make to succeed. Your son or daughter will be handed a long list of assignments, readings, and upcoming exams when they get the syllabi of the courses they have chosen. Without a doubt, this list will be far longer than any they have experienced in high school—even if they have to survive the rigors of AP, IB, or sophisticated coursework from the best independent schools.

If they keep their high school mentality, they likely will plow through this material with diligence and seriousness. They might think that to be serious they need to read every word, do every problem, memorize every concept. As following the instructions of teachers has gotten them a long way—into a good college—they are likely to apply this principle to their new campus. They think of their brain like a large bucket. Pour as much as you can into it, and it will all work out.

But this will not work. Mastery is not possible anymore by just memorizing. Simple recall will not answer the questions they will be asked, nor will it work. There simply will be too much to memorize, even if that was what was required. An Organic Chemistry professor at Johns Hopkins University always insisted that memorizing formulas would get his students nowhere, yet many were convinced that was what he wanted and how they should prepare. And then they would fail his exams.

A better, more appropriate approach calls for *strategic thinking* and *self-discipline*, which challenges a student to own his or her education. I have suggested in previous chapters that you encourage your daughter or son to be more self conscious about the purpose of their education. Now, I'm asking you to have them pose similarly tough questions about how they are learning. The act of studying, you should argue, is not a cramming exercise but a thoughtful journey.

I ask them these questions in *Dean's List*: Why am I reading this text? What am I supposed to get out of it? What kinds of questions does it answer? Will I be able to solve a problem based on what I'm doing and practicing? How do these readings and concepts connect to one another? How do they connect with those discussed in lecture?

Whether it is understanding the Hundred Years' War or the dynamics of cellular structures, they will need to pull back from the task of reading or completing problem sets to ask these questions. Only by seeing the big picture, by connecting concepts and applying one idea to another, will they get what the professor is trying to do. And those connections do not come from the "hard" work of absorbing and memorizing, although those are necessary partners in learning. They will come from the "soft" work of thinking, puzzling, and wondering.

In essence, strategic students are not preoccupied with lower levels of cognitive work. They are building higher orders of critical analysis, which demands skepticism, thoughtfulness, and the ability to jump from one idea to another without falling. They are moving from *absorbing* something to *understanding* it. When you talk to your student about how they are studying, ask them directly whether they see any distinction or differences with high school study.

If they don't see that, advise them to ask their professors for tips on how best to study the materials. Professors, unfortunately, do not usually share these tips in their syllabi or discussions. They assume that students are ready to make the transition to strategic studying or that they have already. But freshmen, or first years, like your son or daughter, generally have not. So your child needs to ask, to push for specifics on how to best take notes, how to make sense of the materials, and how to prepare for exams.

Many campuses offer services to help students study more effectively, and you should urge your daughter or son to use them. These services are not tutoring, which focuses on the substance of a course. We called them *study consulting* at Johns Hopkins University. Study consultants were coaches who helped students take better notes, manage their time, and make the transition to strategic thinking and learning. Feel free to suggest these coaches to your child.

Figuring Out the Lecture

Unless your son or daughter has picked a small college, or at least a small academic program, he or she will sit in lectures much of their first year. Lectures vary in size from, say, 30 to more than 1,000 students. Dating from at least the Middle Ages, lectures are a proven (or, at least, common) tool of instruction. They have the distinct advantage of transferring information to students in an efficient, scalable fashion. A professor can deliver the same script, with the same presentation tools or slides, to a few dozen as they do to several hundred.

From a university's perspective, lectures are cost-effective, too. You need only one professor, preferably with enough charisma and funny stories to engage and even entertain large groups of young people. That professor can employ several, even dozens, of teaching assistants to carry the burden of breakout sessions and grading. So you need only one professional and an army of underpaid graduate students to handle what would be a much more expensive enterprise if undergraduates were divided into professor-led courses.

However efficient they may be, lectures are an ironic way to teach in an environment that values critical thinking and complex interconnections. A lecture is a passive experience for the listener, beyond trying to summarize what is happening in hastily written notes. Students naturally try to transcribe all that is said, even when lectures are recorded or when notes or slides are provided afterward.

Many lectures, not surprisingly, only have the appearance of a learning experience. Chances are that your daughter or son is sleeping through it, checking their phone for messages, daydreaming, or taking notes grudgingly. Or they aren't there at all—even when your family is paying thousands for the privilege. Professors do not take attendance, and they know when most of the class isn't showing up after the first meeting.

Talk about the experience of lectures with your daughter or son. Ask them what it feels like, what they are doing, how they are learning in such a large and often intimidating environment. Don't scold them for not asking questions, as that's very hard to do without looking foolish. But you can suggest that they approach lectures by asking questions internally, to engage the material rather than try to absorb it *in toto*.

They can ask these questions from *Dean's List*: How did that idea connect to the one the professor just said? What is the relationship between what she is saying and the readings that I did last night or last week? Where is this course going? How are all of the lectures hanging together conceptually? Is she building some kind of larger argument that I'm not seeing yet? She just told a particular story; was that important? Why did she tell that story? What am I supposed to get from that? I'm not sure what that means—should I?

If they ask questions as they listen, they will begin to see how a lecture can be one side of a dialogue between them and the professor, an engaged conversation rather than a passive data dump. Indeed, if lecture notes are only a summary of what was said, they will be of little use as time passes and memory fades. If those notes include circled areas of confusion, questions written in the columns, exclamation marks when something seems important, and arrows that connect one idea to another, then those notes take on their own meaning. They become a tool for learning, not just a transcript.

You may also suggest that your son or daughter experiment with different note-taking techniques. Again, a study consultant can help with this, as they can see what your daughter is already doing with note-taking and suggest modifications. For our purposes, you can make a few suggestions:

- Get to the lecture early to gather your thoughts and review previous notes.
- Don't write everything down.
- Consciously stop writing occasionally and just listen.
- Write down questions and confusions in the margins.
- Don't leave as soon as the lecture is over. Sit and reflect on what you have heard.

Don't be surprised if you're met with eye-rolling as you make these suggestions. I've already spent most of this guidebook suggesting you back away from daily college life and decision-making. Study techniques are central to success, but they are just techniques, not decisions. By suggesting that your son or daughter be self-conscious about those techniques and pushing them to make their own decisions, you are consistently asking them to own their education in a way that is reflective and strategic, not accidental or poorly considered. It may be a subtle shift in parenting, but a healthy one.

Working Better, Not Working Harder

In Strategies #8 and #9, I will be discussing the rather grim but predictable prospect of failure. Even the best students will struggle from time to time, for reasons as benign as forgetting to submit an assignment to as serious as broken relationships or illnesses. They may have over-committed to other activities or sports, which exposes poor time management and chronic procrastination.

It will be tempting at these moments to urge your daughter or son to work harder. "What's the matter with you? You used to work so hard in high school—hadn't you better just get to work?" As I will argue in Strategy #8, sometimes effort is beside the point, as there are more fundamental problems pulling them down. And sometimes it is the problem, as students become distracted with video games, Netflix, or too many earnest conversations with friends and roommates.

But you can play a healthier role in this mix of explanations and problems than urging them to work harder. That is likely to backfire on you, as they resent your criticism and your attack on their character. They might continue to slide away from hard work just to prove the point that they are in charge. A healthier approach is to ask how they might work *better*. You don't need them to work long hours fruitlessly nor to give up so much of what makes American college life so rich: friendships, service, activities, and fun.

There is no simple formula for studying more productively. Students vary too much in background, skills, expertise, culture, and personality to offer a single path. Your better choice is to support them as they experiment with what works best for them. And do this early, as habits form quickly in the first year. If those habits are not productive, then they will linger and prove a handicap.

Begin with assuring them that college studies are different and therefore need to be learned. Point out that anything new is an opportunity to define it as they like, to tailor it to their needs and style. Urge them to find a new groove, a new set of habits that work in a new environment with a new set of expectations.

If it helps, and you can do this gently, you can suggest more specifics. Try new locations, not just your room, where you may be tempted by other distractions or the comfort of napping. Vary where you are throughout the day, as a change of venue can renew your energy and return your focus. Be honest about your attention span, which may mean you need to study one subject for short bursts. Experiment with different ways to read—for example, skimming, followed by review of key passages. Does it help to study with others, asking one another questions? (Probably.) Try studying without listening to music or watching a video on your other device.

Be careful as you make these suggestions. They may be effective on the merits, but if you push too hard, you will find that your good advice is not only ignored but also flouted by students studying less or intentionally studying poorly. That may be self-defeating, but if they have to do that to make space between you and reestablish their independence, they will.

If you feel them pulling away, back off immediately. The best you can do is to assure them that college is a new challenge and suggest they consult resources, such as getting a study coach or meeting with the professor. The important takeaway is that you show a good faith effort to be supportive without being bossy.

Sleep, Friend of All Students

When your kids are big, and maybe taller than you are, they certainly seem too big to tuck into bed. Now that they are out of the house, tucking in just isn't possible anymore. And who tucks in a grown-up?

But they aren't all grown-up. They are late adolescents. And they need much more sleep than they are getting. I would put money on that. The anti-sleep culture runs deep on college campuses, powered by coffee, late-night pizzas, the perception of invincibility, peer pressure, loud dormitories—and no parents to tell them to sleep. Yet they need deep, sustained sleep to function on every level.

It doesn't help that they likely have mismanaged time on any given day, likely waiting until after dinner to start studying. They suddenly realize they have five or six hours of work ahead of them, and their bodies and minds are failing just at the moment when memory, concentration, analysis, insight, and creativity are in greatest demand.

Even if you are enlightened parents, happy to let your children make mistakes, make independent decisions, and grow up in the safe confines of a college campus, you have my permission to demand that they get more sleep.

Go ahead and ask them when they got up, when they did their studying, and when they have gotten to sleep. Remind them that looking at screens just before bed makes getting to sleep tougher. Eating too late, getting too little exercise, failing to manage stress all contribute to poor sleep, let alone not enough of it.

This all gets much more challenging for student athletes, whose bodies are recovering from demanding games, matches, or practices.

Late at night, they are just not physically capable of the kind of intellectual engagement required by college-level studies. They have to front-load this work, preferably before practices, and manage their bodies as well as their time—*and* get more sleep.

If you insist on one thing, insist on sleep.

Around the Kitchen Table

Parenting a successful college student is complicated because there is no one pattern to follow. On the one hand, you need to give them space to grow. On the other hand, there are some important issues you should discuss. In Strategy #6, I make the argument that an open conversation about the changing demands of studying is a discussion worth having.

Without being heavy-handed, you can ask how your daughter or son is managing the new workload, the changing expectations of professors, the newness of lectures, and the crazy pace of a day that stretches long into the night—leaving them deprived of the sleep their bodies crave.

Listen for resignation, defensiveness, stress, and weariness. You're likely very familiar with those sounds, and they are still signs that matter. A student who is not well-organized will feel overwhelmed by the workload and needs coaching to restore a sense of control and calm. When they are trying to absorb every detail and formula, they are not acting strategically, and they will feel mastery is impossible. When they are mismanaging the day, postponing work and failing to get real sleep, their systems will shut down.

So that is why a good, frank conversation about the basic issues of managing life in college is worthwhile, even if it's interfering. By pressing on these questions, you are focusing on the means to whatever ends they may want. You're not telling them where to go. You're pointing out that getting there will be difficult without the basics of time management, insightful approaches to learning, and a good night's sleep. You already know how to insist on this, so go ahead.

➡️ ∗ Are you comfortable with what your professors are expecting from you? Do you understand those expectations?

* I know you may be feeling that, if you're having a tough time, you're not working hard enough. Are you sure that's the problem? Could you be working too hard on the wrong things?
* Do you know where to go to get help on studying? Start with the Academic Advising Office. I'm sure they could tell you what to do.
* Are you feeling overwhelmed at all? When do you feel that way? What do you think is happening then?
* How well are you sleeping? What can you do to make that sleep better for you?
* Are you getting enough sleep? Can you change some things to help?

Invite Them to
Be Uncomfortable

When colleges look at the world, and they see ethnic and geographic diversity, they see an opportunity for learning. Such a world, characterized by ever-changing blends of peoples and cross-national movements, is complicated, confusing, and messy. It pushes us out of comfortable tribes and clans, and demands that we face people who are different from us. They speak another language, wear different clothing, worship in ways that seem odd, and hold values that conflict with our worldview. This world may be profoundly disorienting, even disturbing. And colleges love that.

Universities and colleges in the United States expend a lot of energy magnifying these trends and conditions. They aggressively recruit students that represent a wide range of economic circumstances, geographic locations, and ethnic identities. Colleges are disappointed when they fail, at the very least, to replicate the wider demographics of race, ethnicity, and gender. They take pride in attracting and admitting students from as many states and countries as they can. Just look at their Web sites—those demographic goals are front and center.

They don't do this expensive and complicated exercise just for appearances. They may like to see a diverse student body, but what they really have in mind is a bit of social engineering. By self-consciously constructing a rich tapestry of experiences and values, they are imitating and anticipating a world that is blended, open, and complex. More importantly, they are creating a provocative learning environment in which students will have to learn, cope, mediate, and celebrate diversity—not fear it.

As you prepare to send your son or daughter to college, or if you have already, you need to make a choice. Do you send them with the confident message that this diversity is an amazing laboratory of intercultural respect? Or not? Do you want to help prepare them for lives in a new reality of open borders and mixed communities? Or not? Do you want them to be challenged by this environment, shifting from suspicion to trust? Or not?

I have difficulty accepting any of these answers in the negative. I have traveled to nearly fifty countries and lived on three continents. My career has been focused on international exchange, and I have served some of the most diverse student bodies in the world. I see the joy and delight in complexity, though I respect the discomfort of those that feel otherwise.

So let me set aside cultural politics and focus on the mission of this guidebook and *Dean's List*: to help your student succeed. I simply believe, from years of experience, that students cannot succeed without embracing the mission of intercultural exchange. They cannot take full advantage of a carefully engineered social environment, nor can they mature intellectually, without making the difficult and uncomfortable choice of learning from diversity. Just as important, finding ways to navigate cultural conflict and value clashes will prepare them well for any professional environment where disagreements arise for many of the same reasons.

And that is why Strategy #7 is *Invite Them to Be Uncomfortable*.

Getting Them Ready

It's possible that these challenges, and the advantages of facing them, are already familiar and natural to your family. You may now live in a diverse neighborhood or city. You may have experienced cross-national movement, inter-racial dialogue, and the need to find common ground with people who appear to be different at first glance. And that will serve your son or daughter well. But maybe not.

Either way, it's healthy to start a conversation about what they will experience or are already seeing and feeling. They may be watching campus conflicts over race identity and disrespect—conflicts that consumed many campuses in 2015 and 2016. They may be confused by the many ethnic-based groups on campus, such as the Korean-American Students Association or the Black Student Union. They may have never seen girls with their heads covered or wondered how one campus could have so many kinds of worship services. Who is "the other" on campus? Who else is there? What does that look like? Is it strange to feel that, maybe now, your daughter or son is a minority?

It's important for you to know that identity and self-meaning are in great flux for college students. They are wondering who they are and what that means, just at the moment when they are seeing a complex demographic environment around them. And those two interact, as they search for identity in contrast to, and in synchrony with others. "Who is the 'other' now?" It's a good question.

In *Dean's List*, I challenge students to cope with questions like this in three steps. You can support these steps by asking good questions when you see them for a break or a campus visit: build awareness, get educated, and initiate dialogue.

Build Awareness

Many college campuses make this first step pretty easy. In the first days on campus, freshmen will be bombarded with campaigns to get involved in many activities and clubs. The most dramatic of these will be an activities fair, where groups will be at tables, yelling at wandering students to check them out and join. Urge your daughter or son to take advantage because being involved is crucial to success, as I've argued. Commitments like intramural sports and musical groups not only expand their experience and circle of friends but also impose discipline on time management. When you have only 76 minutes until rehearsal, rather than 4 hours before bed, you're more likely to be focused and productive.

But there is another reason to wander that fair. Your son or daughter should see it, in part, as a spectacle, a demonstration of the diversity and variety on the campus. They can note that there are many nationality- or ethnic-based groups, like the Filipino American Club. They should also take a moment to savor how different students are from one another. There is complexity and beauty in such a moment, as jarring and confusing as that might be. It can be hard to process that complexity, but there can be no processing without awareness of it. That fair can be a start.

Suggest to your student that reading the school newspaper and watching campus politics can be a healthy way to appreciate diversity and the conflict that can result. They can learn about the recent history of their campus. Have there been protests or petitions over racial equality and respect? What has been the response to those actions? College campuses such as Yale and the University of Missouri have been roiled by these conflicts. It is no coincidence that the violence and turmoil resulting from white supremacist marches in Charlottesville took place near the campus of the University of Virginia in 2017.

Campuses have had to face the reality that the outward appearance of intellectual equality and engagement may be masking deeply felt disrespect, misunderstanding, and anger. Your daughter or son should not look the other way when seeing this conflict, but embrace it as a challenge to their own identity, values, and perspective.

When I was a dean at Johns Hopkins University, a fraternity hosted a Halloween party they foolishly called "Halloween in the 'Hood." The party featured sounds of gunfire and crime scenes. The African American community on campus was outraged, with good reason, but the incident became a trigger for difficult conversations and confrontations about widely felt racism. This confused many students and (admittedly) administrators who had thought all was well when, in fact, students of colors felt marginalized and disrespected.

It can be difficult to accept these feelings and realities, particularly if you consider yourself enlightened or accepting. Professors who live by open exchange and intellectual respect can react defensively when told they are not the virtuous, accepting citizens they imagined themselves to be. And a student like your son or daughter can ricochet from denial to defensive anger to confusion to empathy.

These feelings may be hard to handle, which provides an opening for you to initiate conversation. Follow the news on campus. College newspapers all are online, usually without subscription. If the campus is going through these challenges, raise this when you check in with your son or daughter. What's happening? How do you feel about that?

Challenge them to learn more about what the racial and ethnic politics are on their campus. Awareness requires some exposure and risk to new ideas and feelings. You should reassure them that it will not be easy to handle—but a worthwhile and crucial part of their college education.

Get Educated

Awareness of diversity issues is common on today's college campus. That, as I've argued, is their intent as they construct a student body. But they do not make this effort nor invest resources around it just to create a conflicted, complicated campus culture. That is only the precondition to education. So, just as awareness grows among students, faculty are there to help make sense of it.

Remember that my advice to parents when your son or daughter is choosing coursework is not to back off and have no role. Final decisions, I have argued, belong to them if only to give them the ownership they need over their intellectual journey. When they own it, when they follow it to satisfy their needs and curiosity, they are more likely to succeed. Even if these particulars belong to them, you can support the goal of being learned by suggesting that they supplement their core coursework with classes that address issues of ethnicity, racial identity, and religious difference. History, sociology, political science, and especially anthropology departments will offer many courses in these fields.

There will be other choices, too. Many campuses offer an intersession or winter term featuring short courses, often for credit without grades. This can create a low-impact opportunity to take a course on the African diaspora, the history of immigration, or ethnic conflict in contemporary Europe. Similar opportunities will cover the college's calendar, as visiting speakers—politicians, authors, activists, clergy—come to campus. Most universities and colleges take full advantage of these visitors, scheduling smaller get-togethers to allow students to ask questions and engage in conversation.

You may have no direct effect on your daughter's or son's choices. They may do none of these things, avoiding these issues for fear of conflict or discomfort. I can understand that. A college sends conflicting signals about whether it should be a safe place to grow or a conflicted and challenging environment to resolve. But you are sending a clear signal when you remain steady in suggesting, gently and only occasionally, that they take the opportunity to process identity and diversity issues with the support and tutoring of faculty. You are saying these issues matter. They exist and require attention in ways that are backed by the discipline and empiricism of the academy. And learning systematically how to cope with these issues will equip them well for a world that can only become more complex and confusing. And that's a good way to define success.

Initiate Dialogue

So what's the point of all this? There is, in fact, no point to being aware of or educated about diversity challenges if this does not lead to understanding, respect, and empathy—to better human relationships. And you can't have those relationships, of course, without initiating them and talking about these challenges. Again, you have a role to play here, albeit from a distance, encouraging your son or daughter to be emotionally daring, to risk feeling foolish or clumsy, and to engage in challenging conversations about identity and conflict.

This is hard to do outside the confines of classrooms or college-organized activities, such as town halls and guest speaker events. So that's a good place to start. Students grasp quickly that they are invited to start those conversations within those confines. That's the point of staging them. Asking tough questions in a seminar on race is not just expected. It's required for a good grade. In these venues, people are expecting provocation. It's why these events are exciting because there is risk, even danger, as raw feelings are exposed and honesty revealed.

But most students are not bold enough to take on tough issues in a public forum. That's why they invented dormitories. These are places of friendship and challenge, creating the artifice of proximity to push students to get to know one another. And that requires some daring, vulnerability, and exposure in a relatively safe environment. With your support, your son or daughter may find the courage to ask a student who dresses and acts differently to explain those differences, to teach them about their lives, faiths, and identities. The word *why* may be the best word, and students should use it as often as they can.

If they can gain some confidence in taking such risks, they will also see that the landscape around them is shifting. Late adolescents are revising themselves all the time. They are exploring racial and sexual identities. They are trying to find wider meaning in their choices. They are trying to figure out what is comfortable and real. So the conversations they have can speak to changes, too. "I noticed you started wearing ___. What's going on?" Appearances may not change, but moods can, so just asking how people are feeling or what is changing for them can open dialogue to many issues.

All of this might seem like a distraction to you from the core purpose of a college education. If you're thinking they are there to become chemists, say, then you have missed the point of an American education. Colleges and universities in the United States are engineered to raise issues and develop young people far beyond the rigors of a course of study. Those same courses of study can follow that path by provoking difficult issues like those raised in this chapter. Colleges have put students in an artificial environment of proximity and society to push them to grow through their friendships and conversations.

You can help them take full advantage of that environment by urging them to be open to the new and the different, to get help from faculty to process these experiences, and to experiment in their relationships to apply those lessons.

Study Abroad

American colleges have an insular, protected feel to them. "Ivy-covered walls" promote a sense of security and comfort—issues of diversity notwithstanding. They create an environment that allows late adolescents to become young adults safely. As this chapter has suggested, colleges break that spell by engineering a provocatively diverse environment, a place where some level of discomfort and misunderstanding will prompt healthy, educated conversations about identity and our place in the world.

Despite these efforts, a campus will always be a special, otherworldly place. And while this is fun and nurturing, it is ultimately misleading. A very large and complex world waits beyond those walls. Adventure awaits, my dad taught me, and studying abroad is an exceptionally powerful and effective way to embrace that adventure. Going out into the world, within the parameters of an academic program, is both intensely educational and strictly necessary in a world where economic borders fall daily even when cultural and political borders seem to grow.

As a parent, you can be the most powerful advocate for this opportunity, and your support can give your daughter or son what will likely be a life-altering experience. They may not get another chance to drink deeply from an international adventure, limited to business trips trapped in a foreign office building, or absorbed by a tourist's thin view of reality. Yet the prospect may be scary or daunting, so your reassurance will be important. How can you do this?

- *Reassure yourself.* You can't support an idea that looks scary or wasteful to you. Do some research on the college's Web site, where you will find many resources on study abroad options. Consider how closely connected the college is to a specific program—is it their faculty or an outside vendor? Look at the size of the program, its academic opportunities, whether your student would live with a family (a great idea with the chance for linguistic immersion) or with other English-speaking students. Learn more about the location, including any security or safety concerns you may have. Once you see that they will be challenged and safe, you will be more comfortable in a role as a booster and supporter.

- *Know the opportunity cost.* If your son or daughter is reluctant to spend any time overseas, learn why. Many times the concern is that they will miss out on important experiences their friends will enjoy. The more you push their thinking and get details, the more likely they are to realize that the trade-off will be worth it, that the time away need not be extended, and that they can return and resume campus life. Academically, it is good to know what classes they would miss while overseas and to know whether requirements can be fulfilled through the study abroad program. Support their efforts to be specific with these costs, knowing that advising and study abroad offices specialize in figuring out how to navigate around or through an international experience.

- *Understand the expenses.* You might assume that a semester or a year abroad will be much more expensive than the same time on campus. You may be right, and you may decide the opportunity is not worth the investment. But don't come to this conclusion too quickly. Study abroad programs vary a great deal financially, and you need to factor all the pieces: airline flights, housing, tuition, sundries, and more. Again, a study abroad office can be quite specific with this. Some programs are significantly less expensive than others. While it may cost more to fly to Brazil than to London, an ecology program in the Amazon is likely less expensive than an international relations course at the London School of Economics, thanks to different costs of instruction and housing. Financial aid always follows students overseas, and there are often additional grants (like the Gilman Scholarship) that can help with expenses.
- *Consider the benefits.* You need to be convinced this is worth it. There is no substitute for full cultural immersion to learn a language. It can be scary, but languages never stick without real use, and there can be no more effective a language laboratory than having to navigate daily life and handle academic challenges in a foreign tongue. Students pushed off campus gain invaluable perspective, a renewed sense of confidence from meeting the challenges, and conviction that they own their education. Many of my returning students suddenly realized they had outgrown campus life and were eager for adventures beyond.

Thinking through the costs, benefits, and challenges of a study abroad experience will help you decide whether and how to be an advocate for the experience. Consistent with other advice I have given you, do this gently. Your insistence on studying abroad may be well-intentioned and educationally sound, but it will backfire as they assert their independence, even at the cost of this amazing opportunity.

You will need to navigate this carefully, offering counterarguments to concerns they voice. They are still looking for reassurance from you, knowing that you have their security and happiness in mind. So supporting a bold international move might surprise them. That's OK. If you surprise them, that moves your relationship forward. They will be glad to know you support prudent risk-taking that helps them grow and learn new skills. And isn't that the point of parenting a successful college student?

Around the Kitchen Table

You have just spent years helping your son or daughter prepare for, apply to, and enroll in a great American college or university. You appropriately focused on academics, pushing them to take challenging courses, insisting that they work hard, and expecting that they produce results. All of this was geared toward preparing them to succeed on that campus. Yet the definition of success continues to challenge both of you, as it is textured and complicated. It isn't measured only by good grades, and it seems to ask for a much wider range of skills and attitudes than you anticipated.

This chapter offers another challenge to that list—how to best take advantage of the diverse environment that the college has engineered to create a provocative and interesting learning environment. That environment might be quite different than anything your child has experienced, and they may find it difficult and confusing, just at the moment when they are struggling with their own sense of self. These are important topics for your kitchen table, topics that go to the heart of a modern American college experience.

I have suggested a path your daughter or son can follow to take advantage of this opportunity: build awareness, get educated, and initiate dialogue. This path is neither simple nor easy, as it demands that they challenge their worldview, their identity, and their value systems. And those have all been shaped by you as their parent. So it is especially powerful, coming from a parent (rather than a faculty member or administrator) that you support a journey along that path. Study abroad is an extension of that path, requiring that you think of their education differently, and your support will be equally powerful there.

It seems odd and seemingly self-defeating for a parent to wish that a son or daughter return from college very different from when they left. Some of that change is the natural order of things, as they grow and mature. But these changes, prompted by diversity and travel, are engineered and self-conscious. So, in encouraging a refreshed look at life, you are pushing them to be different than you are, to believe things that you might not. It may be a gift to push your child from this nest, and it may be uncomfortable, but it demands that we react to those changes without questioning our best efforts to prepare them for life.

* What are you seeing on campus on race relations? Does there seem to be tension between groups? What does that look like?
* Have there been any controversies about racial justice or religious identity? How do those controversies make you feel?
* When you see a posting or an event for an organization like the Chinese American Club or the Black Alliance, what do you think about that?
* I see the college has a "diversity" course requirement. Does that seem like a waste of time? Why or why not?
* Have any of your friends started talking about studying abroad? Does that seem like a good idea? Why or why not? How important is the international experience?
* Have you given any thought to what a semester or year abroad might do for you? Are there some things you can do to prepare?

Know the Signs and Reasons for Failure

This is the tough chapter, so buckle up. It's time to confront the possibility, even the likelihood, of your student's failure. When students struggle and fail in college, their parents understandably sometimes fall apart. We are filled with anxiety and guilt. We start asking questions about how well we raised our children. Did we prepare them well enough? Did we make sure they were healthy? Why did we push them to go to Stanford? Why didn't we know this was happening?

When I was a dean at Johns Hopkins University, my children were not college age. So I watched the heartache of my students' parents with sympathy and concern but not empathy. I did not yet understand the leap of faith that sending a child to college requires. When that leap seems to prove foolish, as our children struggle, we feel betrayal, anger, and anguish. Now I get it, feeling lucky that my son is doing fine, but thinking that (a) I might not know if he is not, and (b) that things could change.

This chapter and the next—and their counterparts in *Dean's List*—address failure, a rarity in books of this kind. You might assume that, if your son or daughter follows the advice of the previous chapters, or similar advice from academic advisors and authors, they will succeed. Of course, I think that is more likely, or I wouldn't be wasting your time and mine. But life, even the relative safety of college life, offers no such guarantees. There are many factors that determine success and failure, and they are worth talking about with your student.

This chapter will shine a harsh light on four reasons for academic struggles and failure. It will be hard for you to read this list, and you may spend much of that time denying that they could affect your daughter or son. Denial is natural, of course, particularly as you have played the most central role in their success to date. If they are failing, then you must be partly responsible, and that's tough to take.

But there is another, important reason why you might set aside these factors as irrelevant. Your son or daughter got into a good college, maybe a great college, overcoming international competition for a precious place on a historic, prestigious, and famous campus. How can they fail after so many years of success? How could things change so much in a matter of months or even weeks?

I'll admit that, when I took over as dean of Advising at Johns Hopkins University, I was surprised to see so many failing students on a top-ranked campus. You would think that Hopkins could pick anyone, guaranteeing success. But it's not that simple there or anywhere else in the realm of prestigious colleges. That's why every college in America has hardworking staff in residential and student life, advising, counseling, health centers, tutoring, and more –all helping students who weren't supposed to fail *but are.*

And every one of those students has a parent or guardian. *You could be one of them.*

Forgive the rhetorical melodrama, but you have to think about this possibility, just as you've identified and handled any number of crises or obstacles your child has faced before. Start with the reassurance that you can handle this one, too, using professional advice and help as you did when your child had an ear infection, trouble with middle school math, a torn ACL from soccer, or challenges with the SAT. You simply name the problem and then treat it.

This chapter outlines Strategy #8, *Know the Signs and Reasons for Failure,* and we do this by naming four major problems for academic struggles and failure:

1. Lack of motivation
2. Poor time management
3. Weak study skills and talent
4. Poor mental and physical health

Lack of Motivation

It's hard to do things if you don't want to do them. This is true for any activity and for anyone. Sure, your son or daughter can be pushed by obligation, by the desire to avoid shame, by expectations, and by simple momentum. But it is not easy, especially when your student is looking up a steep learning curve for a course in chemistry, sociology, neuroscience, or a foreign language. When there is a lot of work to do and no one to hold you accountable, losing motivation is a serious blow to a student and a major contributor to failure.

Burnout is a common cause of failed motivation. You know how hard your son or daughter worked in high school. Too many intense courses, from AP or IB. Too many activities, from band to volunteering. Too many tests. Too many pressures from the college search. Too many expectations to meet from teachers, from friends, from you. Your student may just be exhausted.

Have a conversation with them about how tired they are. Does college seem like another chore, another mountain after climbing many others? How daunting does this seem to them? When you look in their eyes, is there resentment and exhaustion? Are they excited when they talk about their courses and requirements, or is there weariness? You need to get a feel for how deep this burnout might be.

Another set of questions should revolve around grades. I have argued that grades are a hollow motivator, and now is the time for you to worry about that. How much does this seem to be an obsession? Are they self-critical when grades fall short of expectations? How frustrated are they with the marks or grades they are getting? If they are focused on what the professor wants, how unfair his or her grades are, then you have a reason to worry, as that suggests they are obsessing about approval when they need to think about how much they are learning.

You should check your own contributions to these conversations. Think about how much you emphasize grades, as you may be adding to the problem of pleasing others rather than satisfying curiosity. There is no easy way to navigate this, I'm afraid. You played the central role in building their self-esteem by offering praise and encouragement, if you privately worry or acknowledge that you said, "Good job!"

when they didn't really. Your job was to be, as best you could, your daughter's or son's cheerleader.

Their dependency on your approval sets a trap for them. If they look to your approval constantly, you will find them anticipating your preferences rather than trying to assess their own. If the relationship heavily depends on your approval and their compliance, then they will lose crucial motivation because you're not with them on campus or if you disapprove of what they are doing. If they make academic or personal choices that don't square with you, it could be painful and burdensome to continue succeeding without your praise.

Making independent choices might be an initial effort to create distance from you—a natural need for an adolescent—but you may be exacting too high a price from them in your criticism. So, just as they explore separation, you punish them, and that loss of support may undermine their motivation to work and succeed. Please proceed with gentle awareness.

Whatever the fundamental causes for lost motivation, it is worth knowing what the symptoms look like. I knew many pre-medical students at Johns Hopkins, because the university attracts so many of them. They carried significant emotional burdens, pressures to succeed and get good grades in their pre-med studies. I would estimate that only one in four of them went on to medical school, and much of that drop-off was caused by the realities of lost motivation for courses they did not find interesting. They only took them because they were required by medical schools or for majors—biology, neuroscience, biomedical engineering—that seemed crucial for admission to medical schools.

When they find these courses boring, when the courses are only an obligation and burden to be gotten out of the way, most students begin to feel intense resentment. Their studies—textbooks, assignments, lab reports, exams—all begin to generate anger and avoidance. They postpone and procrastinate because the very thought of studying for an organic chemistry test is intimidating, off-putting, and disheartening. They create a cycle of worry and failed expectations, compounding the worries and leading to more resentment and avoidance.

When students start hating their studies, when learning is a burden, they lose motivation. They avoid the work. They don't push through when assignments are difficult. They don't make the needed effort or practice problems. They don't ask questions, attend class, seek tutoring, or arrange study groups.

And then they fail.

Managing Time Poorly

Recall some of the arguments I made in the introduction on the difference between high school and college. From your vantage point, the main difference is that your son or daughter is not in your house or apartment anymore. Their lives are simply unplugged from your routine. And the visibility you had, however limited, of how they spent their time has now disappeared. You watched them come and go. You drove them to practice or performances. You fed them breakfast and waited up when they went out on weekends. Now, poof! They're gone. You're living your life, and their time is theirs.

From your daughter's or son's vantage point, the world has changed radically. While your world is likely the same, if lonelier because of their absence, theirs looks nothing like high school. Time is an ocean stretching before them, without edges, without structure, without limit. True, they have classes to attend. But the amount of time in class is a fraction of that in high school, and (for the most part) they don't have to attend. No one is watching them, shepherding them from one activity or one class to another. There is no designated study hall (except for some athletes) or pattern to when they should study. Students vary greatly in when they do that, so there's no readily available model or pattern to follow. Floating in this ocean is an opportunity for procrastination. Students let the day float away (to mix water metaphors), waiting until they are too tired, late at night, to get anything done—without the capacity to remember or think clearly.

What are they doing with all that potentially productive time? It may be easy as a parent to see studying as productive and other choices as poor, but there are a lot of great, productive activities on a campus. They can join an orchestra, edit the school newspaper, lead a sorority, organize a charity fund-raiser, play varsity basketball, and sing in the glee club. These are all worthy activities. Indeed, without committing to co-curricular activities, students lose all the structure to their days. A healthy balance of singing and playing make students more productive as their time becomes limited in more predictable ways.

The issue to understand is what is most important to them, and what gives them the most satisfaction. If you've gone to college primarily to play football, and football is the main pleasure in your life, then even the limited time you have left to study will be a resentful chore. If you have chosen a course of study to please your parents and come with shaky skills, you may be in full avoidance of those studies, allowing all your other activities to fill your time.

Of course, your daughter or son can waste their time with pointless activities—video games, binge-watching Netflix, surfing the Web, posting on Snapchat. Everyone deserves a break from the difficult and the monotonous. It's healthy. However, there are decidedly unhealthy pastimes, such as drinking, drugs, online gambling, and obsessive relationships.

Time is everyone's most precious and fleeting resource; yet, college students often think that time is unlimited, seeing little harm in wasting it. Eventually, they have to put the work in to maintain any success. But by pushing those times into places when they are tired or rundown, generally late at night, they are fighting their brains' and bodies' craving for rest. They are trying to absorb and understand when they are least able to do that. If drugs or alcohol are part of procrastination, studying will be even more futile.

And then they fail.

Weak Study Skills and Talent

In Strategy #7, I pointed out that universities work hard to assemble a diverse student body, hoping this is provocative and educational. That is intentional. What admissions offices try to avoid is admitting a student body whose academic skills vary too much. Colleges set high standards for high school grades and tests precisely to avoid this problem. They want a reliable and capable student body, ready to take on the challenges their faculty set. That goal is good for everyone. Faculty can push everyone equally, starting from a similar starting gate. And the college makes sure everyone graduates, which is good for their reputation, national ranking, and financial bottom line.

But accomplishing this is not simple. First, no group of students ever has the exact same levels of study skills. They could all come from the same, elite prep school, even from the same teacher, and they would vary from one another. No college would want that homogeneity anyway. Now imagine the intellectual chaos and the variation in skill if you recruit from all 50 states and 30 countries, from every socioeconomic group, and from dozens of cultures. Add to that the need for the college to populate sports teams and orchestras, English and physics departments, and still have gender, racial, and ethnic balance. And you have a student body with a lot of variation in how well prepared they are for college.

As a parent, you can't assume, therefore, that just because your student got into a good school that they are fully prepared to handle it academically. Your daughter or son might be missing important skills. For example, a lot of students coming from larger public schools have not been given the attention they need to become college-level writers. Good writing requires practice and detailed feedback. A teacher with more than 100 students cannot handle that amount of grading.

Your son or daughter may take notes poorly. He or she may not know how to construct an argument or use a source properly. They may not have needed to spend more than a few hours a day on their studies. So they don't have the organizational skills to prepare for exams that now come just twice a semester.

It is hard to appreciate the possibility that your child is not well-prepared. But it will be harder to accept that she or he may not have the *talent* to succeed in a particular area of study. However hard she works, your daughter may not be able to learn a foreign language at a college level. Your son may not "get" Organic Chemistry—a lot of people don't. You love your college student, but that might obscure your ability to see that she or he doesn't have a talent for everything you think they do.

A lack of skill or a talent might not have consequences, but it usually does. Many students choose a course of study for reasons other than how well it fits their skills and talents. They think they need to major in biology, overlooking that they haven't the skills to make sense of the reams of details required in biology courses. They may not see they lack the talent to handle the major's required courses in chemistry and physics. But they keep to the plan because it's the plan.

And then they fail.

Poor Health

I have left the most troubling contributor to student failure for last—their physical and mental health. It's disquieting to parents because their health has been so fundamental to your role. Keeping them healthy in every way has been your responsibility and burden from the beginning. And now you can't watch over them.

You don't really know when they go to bed, so you can't tell if they're getting enough sleep. You can't control their dormitory environment, so you can't be sure they have a quiet, clean, and comfortable place to get better sleep. You might be paying for their meals, but you're not there to be sure they eat vegetables and a salad. Sugary cereals and soda may never be in your pantry, but they're at every college cafeteria in America.

You had some sense of whether your son or daughter used drugs or drank while they were in high school—though this can always be hard to detect. Now you can't monitor their behavior. The 21-year-old drinking age is meaningless in a college town. Fraternities and sororities take full advantage of their reputation to encourage drinking. College students don't drink for taste; they drink for effect. And your daughter or son is likely part of that culture. But you can't know how serious this is until it is too late.

More troubling is the thought that their mental health will have a profound effect on their studies and success. College campuses have been challenged by a wave of mental illnesses: depression, bipolar diseases, eating disorders, and many forms of anxiety. Many of these illnesses and conditions manifest themselves in college. They could have left home just fine and developed a condition on campus. Or they may have been misdiagnosed. Or you may know these challenges, helped to treat them, but now can't see whether that treatment is continuing successfully.

I have known many students who carry their mental health challenges like a heavy stone. They are determined and strong, doing their best to manage their lives, studies, and health at once. But they buckle when one of these three takes on greater weight, from a difficult course to relationship gone wrong. They're not getting enough sleep. They become increasingly anxious and distracted. They can't focus no matter what they do. Their efforts are inadequate for overcoming the barriers before them.

And then they fail.

Around the Kitchen Table

And then they fail.

And then they fail.

And then they fail.

Grim stuff. Difficult to handle. Unexpected and awful. Yet these causes for failure are common and real. No book focused on success should avoid the possibility of failure. Failure is not just an absence of successful strategies. It is a human reality that has many causes. Any parent is tough enough to acknowledge this, so I'm giving it to you straight.

I have spent much of this chapter underscoring how difficult it is to know whether any of these four major problems are apparent. How do you know whether they've lost motivation, failed to manage time well, stopped eating and sleeping well, and become depressed? They are not living at home, so it's hard to know. To make matters worse, colleges have put up a series of roadblocks to your visibility. They won't share what they know to respect both US federal law that ensures student privacy and to follow their own culture of student independence.

So what can you do to find out whether anything is going wrong? *You can ask.* This is not a perfect answer to this question, as your daughter or son can conceal these problems from you, which they may do to assert their independence or because they are embarrassed. They may underestimate a problem and its impact. Or your relationship may not be open or comfortable enough to trust you with that news.

But you must try in a way that is gentle but insistent. Don't accept a simple "Oh, I'm fine" from them. Follow up with more specifics. Rely on the questions that follow. Try to balance their increasing need for privacy and independence with your need for both reassurance and information. (I will discuss what to do with that information in the next chapter.)

Those conversations may validate your concerns. Your fears may have real merit, and you can see that you need to know more. Again, be conservative in reaching that conclusion, but listen to your instincts. In that case, you may want to get the cooperation of the college to know what is happening. That will require the consent of your son or daughter, who would need to waive in writing their privacy rights, opening their files to you. I offer this advice reluctantly, as taking this step is a serious, irreversible intrusion into your student's development as an adult. But if their health and safety are at risk, it is a choice you may need to make.

Even if you don't go that far, you need to remain sharp and observant. This will be hard to do, as many changes will be perfectly normal. Ask questions, even if they are obvious, leading, or even prying. Remain curious and concerned. Remember there is a difference between making decisions for them, which respects their independence, and making sure they are healthy and clear of trouble. If you do, you're more likely to catch failure before it spreads.

* I'm betting college is more difficult than you and your friends might have expected. Do you know anyone who is having a hard time? What are they going through? How does that make you feel?
* It must be strange to have so much unstructured time. Have you figured out what to do with all that? Do you feel a little at sea? Maybe unsure how to manage?
* What does it feel like when you struggle or fail? What are you thinking when that happens? What happens next? How do you react?
* Are you and your friends surprised when you have academic problems? Why do you think you would be surprised?
* Are there some classes in which you have a tough time even

getting started on your studies? You know what it's like to procrastinate, but for those classes, is there something specific that stops you from working?

* I know the end of high school and all the college search stuff was exhausting. Is it difficult to restart that engine?

* You said you were "disappointed," even embarrassed, by your grades. What were you expecting and was that fair to you? You're "falling short" but to whom?

* Do you ever realize in the middle of the day, "Wait, I've wasted the whole thing?" Why did that happen? Can you remember what you did instead?

* Everybody needs a break and some fun. When does that happen for you?

* I know lots of college students drink and experiment with drugs. Some get hooked. Have you been worried about anybody?

* Do you feel like you're in over your head in any of your courses? Why do think that's happening?

* Are there subjects that make you feel good and smart? Are there others that make you feel slow or clumsy?

* Are you getting enough sleep? Why not? Starting too late? Dorm too loud? Roommate annoying? Maybe you're worried about things. You want to talk about that?

* Anything really distracting you from your work? Anything make you feel out of control or without focus? Anybody you know having problems with depression?

* Are you getting to class? Or maybe feeling bad or something like, "what's the point?"

Help Them to Forgive Themselves and Rebuild

I t's a Sunday afternoon in February. You are sitting on cold bleachers at a county recreation facility, watching your daughter play basketball. Her team is struggling, but they're making a comeback late in the second half. Your daughter has the ball at the top of the key and sees an opening. She drives to the basket and is fouled. So she goes to the foul line for two shots. Bench players are yelling, parents are cheering. She knows these two baskets could make the difference in the game and continue the momentum. She senses the tension among her teammates on the court.

She misses the first free throw. It doesn't even hit the rim. Airball.

You clench your teeth, distressed for her, upset she missed the shot so badly, feeling the pressure on her. You hold your breath because you know she's thinking about that miss. She's always been tough on herself, and now the weight of the team is on her, the whole building is watching her, and she needs to make the second free throw. She hates making mistakes, and while this is not really a mistake, it feels that way. And she has to repeat the exact same motion, hoping for a different outcome.

Does she forgive herself and move on? Or does her mind go dark, losing confidence and fulfilling her expectation to fail again?

In a way, moments like these define our children and challenge us as parents. We know that life will hit them with many setbacks and failures, minor and significant. We understand that many of their childhood and classroom experiences tried to teach them how to rebound from such failures. Do they get down on themselves, frustrated, and angry? Do they prematurely conclude they can't do something? Or do they learn and grow with resilience—one of humanity's best qualities.

You have just read Strategy #8, *Know the Signs and Reasons for Failure*, outlining several powerful forces that can derail your son's or daughter's college success. Many of them challenge their emotional balance and their sense of self. And all of these forces demand renewal and change to escape their influence and to rediscover the academic success that propelled your son or daughter to college in the first place. Do they find a way to get help, to regroup, and to forgive themselves?

That is why Strategy #9, *Help Them to Forgive Themselves and Rebuild*, is so important. On one level, your daughter or son has an immediate, pressing job to do: get back on track. To whatever degree they are experiencing failure—from a single failed exam to academic withdrawal from college—they need to fix what's wrong.

But on a more enduring level, they need to find ways to recover from life's ongoing blows. You can support them in important ways, just as you have throughout their childhood. It's only that you now have the obstacles of distance and respect for their growing independence.

Helping Them Rediscover Motivation

Let's look at these challenges in the same order as you found them in Strategy #8. Rediscovering the motivation to learn, and to enjoy the learning process, is profoundly important for struggling students. You can be instrumental to this thinking, but first, you have to let go of at least two things. First, you have to abandon the illusion that they are doing just fine. This can be hard to do, as it means accepting that their failure is real. If your first instinct is to say, "Oh, you'll be fine, just work a little harder," you may be perpetuating the problems—albeit unintentionally. Better to tell them that struggle is natural and common. There is no dishonor in making mistakes. In fact, strength and character come from overcoming mistakes. Help them find the positive in the real.

Second, you may have to let go of the plan—the course of study, the major, the profession—all those small and large expectations that existed before now. You need to be open to endorsing letting go of expectations, as this obligation may be the source of the problem. Your students may be failing because either they don't want to follow the plan, exhibiting simple passive aggression against it, or they just can't handle what the plan requires.

You both may agree that engineering is a good choice, but if they can't manage Calculus III, even with a lot of help, then you need to relieve them of the pressure to complete the plan. The plan may need to be tabled for a while and revived in some fashion. But relieving the pressure and expectations will allow them to recapture their own internal motivation to learn.

If you can clear the table emotionally, then you can suggest one of several strategies for finding their motivation. First, help them understand, as I've argued in Strategy #5, *Disconnect Majors and Careers*, that careers and majors are not the same thing. If they dream of being a lawyer or a doctor, there are many ways to reach that goal, freeing them to choose a course of study that appeals to their natural curiosity and interests, rather than to some dreaded requirement.

Second, invite them to explore more choices. If they are not finding anything interesting, it's likely because (a) they have defined "interesting" as something familiar that they can explore with confidence, or (b) they haven't looked. Most educational systems seem intent on replacing the innate curiosity of children with the drudgery of requirements and obligations. Years of tedious study replace the joy of discovery with the fleeting satisfaction of good grades.

Now you have to help reverse that, reminding them that learning is more important than pleasing others. If they're getting failing grades, they are not pleasing others (their instructors and you), so that approach isn't working anyway. You need to support a new approach, where they look for subject matter that pleases, excites, and satisfies them.

There are lots of ways they can find better choices.

- *Keep an open mind.* They can set aside their ignorance of a subject, like anthropology or botany, and learn more about that subject with an open mind. Just because the label is unfamiliar or the brand of the discipline is boring or impractical should not stop them from looking.

- *Explore the bookstore.* Students use bookstores and Web sites in such limited, utilitarian ways. You need a book, you get a book. But both resources offer the chance to browse, to look around, to read a few paragraphs. At a physical bookstore, the textbooks are just waiting there for your son or daughter to open them up and see what's inside.
- *Explore department Web sites.* Academics are terrible at marketing. But these Web sites do have untapped resources for students. They can learn about the discipline, what faculty are researching, what programs the department offers, and whether there are scholarships or special projects available to them.
- *Talk to people.* What is the point of living on a campus if you don't take advantage of personal access to a diverse learning community? Remind your daughter or son that there are lots of people around campus who love their studies. The faculty, of course, love their disciplines or they wouldn't be faculty. How about roommates, teammates, orchestra partners, friends? Surely, someone is having fun. Their choices may not fit your student's interests, though they could, but sometimes talking to someone who has found a happy academic home proves that you can find such a home.
- *Leave campus.* You may not want to hear this advice, but sometimes students need to leave college to rediscover their own motivation and sense of wonder. Maybe that can be found at a soup kitchen or a food pantry near home. Maybe on an internship at a local museum. Maybe a trip to a new city or even a distant country can raise questions that reignite curiosity. This tactic may stretch your patience and drain your wallet, but it is a sound investment if your struggling student needs to learn that learning is marvelous.

Finally, have an honest and open discussion about why they went to college in the first place. This might be a tough conversation, as you both may admit that the reasons were pretty shallow. Maybe you both thought it was the best way to get a specific job. Or because it's something everyone does. Or it's something your family has dreamed of but never specified why. Or you agree that, just because they have always done well academically, and in a particular field of study, they will continue along the same path.

Now that failure or struggle has interrupted that path, is that field of study right? If it is, how does he or she succeed with it? If it is not, what other courses of study are more appealing, friendly, and, frankly, easier?

Conversations like these matter to supporting a successful student. Continue to challenge yourself to be positive and less judgmental. Motivation or its absence is a root cause for success and failure in all walks of life. More important than getting them back on track is helping them learn how to recover, how to rediscover joy and a sense of mission. This is a lesson they will reuse throughout life. So proceed gently. Back off when you've struck a nerve, and find a better time to talk.

Encouraging Better Time Management

You likely spent most of your teenager's life arguing with them about how they use or misuse their time. How they managed their many commitments—soccer practice, baseball games, homework, volunteer time, family chores—affected you directly, as you likely did the driving, cooking, washing, and more. You discovered, then, that they loved to avoid anything they disliked, from cleaning their room to starting a social studies project.

Now you have reason to believe that they're still wasting time, though you can't say for sure. To have an effect on their time management is not easy. It is problematic, as life management is their responsibility as a maturing adult. Again, you'll have to navigate this carefully. *Dean's List* offers some suggestions:

- *Do nothing.* It can be revealing to sit somewhere and do nothing when you really need to do something else. In this case, they need to get to work. There are assignments, readings, and class preparation in front of them. If they would rather not do that, suggest that they just sit there doing nothing at all. Boredom will overcome them, and preparing for a Spanish test now suddenly seems worthwhile.
- *Track what they are doing.* At Johns Hopkins University, advisors had a lot of success with students who did not manage time well by asking them (a) to chart how they expected to use their time and (b) to chart how they actually used their time. Compar-

ing these two charts inescapably revealed how time was wasted, prompting a lot of students to reexamine their priorities.

- *Treat studying like a job.* When you have a job, you have to show up on time, stay focused on your duties, and then go home. If your daughter or son can think about their work as a job, with that structure and expectations, they are more likely to remain focused and on target. With that day's work done early, thanks to that focus, they can go home and relax.

These techniques work, but really any conversation about time is a challenge to your student to take charge of their lives. Invited to be independent by the culture of college, they have the chance to author their lives, and time management is the most obvious way to do that. You should not tell them what is important or lecture them that their studies should matter. They know that; it's obvious.

What you can express is (a) the knowledge that poor motivation will weaken their resolve to work and (b) that simply thinking through how they use time will help them find their own productive rhythm. You're there to support them, even when they're struggling, not order them to be smart about time.

Showing Them How to Strengthen Their Skills

When students struggle in college, parents can take on the guilt of allowing their students to prepare poorly for college. The line between high school preparation and college life is not straight or even clear, much as we would like it to be. There are many roads through college, and it can be difficult to prepare for them all, even with a wide-ranging set of high school courses. Indeed, a strength of the American high school system is the commitment to be broadly exposed to different subjects. But when a history or physics professor in college sets expectations, they often do that focused on their own discipline, and that can be jarring.

As you consider conversations with your struggling daughter or son, help them to focus on several questions. You'll find these questions should lead, as you can suggest, to getting help from the faculty, teaching assistants, and support services, such as tutoring.

- *Are you taking good notes?* The art of note-taking is complex, as students learn in Strategy #6 of *Dean's List* on working smart. They need to be thoughtful about what role their notes play, which is much more than a transcription of what they are seeing. Many colleges have a "study consulting," or "study skill," program in which students can work with a study coach who looks at their notes and guides them to more effective techniques.

- *Are you thinking about* how *you read?* Reading in college is not the same thing as opening your brain and pouring information into it. There is a level of intellectual interactivity that your son or daughter needs to grasp, where he or she asks questions of the material. Again, a study consultant can help, but talking to the course's professor can be more effective. The professor, in office hours, can suggest ways to focus on key points within a reading, rather than trying to remember it all.

- *What is the professor saying about optional assignments?* At the risk of intrusiveness, you should know that many courses have optional readings and assignments. When a student finds a course difficult, she or he can often overcome that by solving more problems, doing an extra reading, or practicing more. Teaching assistants can work with your student to identify what optional or additional work could help.

- *Are you OK with getting help?* You must reassure your student that getting help is why they are in college or university in the first place. If they had the skills and expertise colleges offer already, there would be no point in attending college. Students attend college to learn, which is another way of asking for help in gaining knowledge. Getting extra help, then, is just an extension of the learning process. Help your student understand that getting a tutor, visiting office hours with good questions, doing extra exercises, and attending optional study sessions are not just OK they are a smarter, deeper way to take advantage of the college's resources and commitment to student success.

- *Have you visited your professor for office hours?* This is always intimidating, even on small, friendly campuses. Professors set aside posted times each week to be available, by drop in or by appointment, to help students. *Dean's List* offers some tactics here, grounded in the idea that preparation, armed with good, specific questions, always helps. Professors are busy and need your student's help to understand the problem. So your daughter or son needs to prepare with references to notes, key passages, and questions from lectures.

- *Have you thought about a study group?* Students often avoid these groups because it forces them to openly express confusion, needs, or questions, when they would rather look confident and strong to their peers. But, once assembled, a well-run group becomes a safe place for intellectual vulnerability. They can ask those questions, divide the challenges, and support one another emotionally.

- *What are we missing here?* "Talent" is a tough concept, unforgiving and unfairly distributed. We all have a loose mixture of talents, and they do not always match our choices particularly well. You may need to play a crucial role in releasing your child from obligations that you likely helped create. If they don't have a talent for language or economics, let them try other fields. Sure, they could try to work harder and push through, but eventually you may need to pivot to encourage the kind of exploration discussed in Strategy #4, *Appreciate Their Academic Choices.* You may need to gently suggest there may be areas they enjoy more and, frankly, seem to understand more readily.

These can be tough conversations to have, requiring the supportive touch I urge you to find. You may need to remind them that forgiving themselves of poor, ill-fitting choices is important to their academic life, as it is for life beyond college. Widening the conversation to include larger issues will be powerful if you set a positive tone.

Urging Them to Take Care of Themselves

You have always been there for your daughter or son, caring for their health since before they were born. From good nutrition to vaccinations, from dental visits to annual checkups, from kissing boo-boos to taking them to an orthopedic surgeon, you have supervised their health.

And now, once again, you feel the powerlessness of distance and ignorance. Mental and physical health challenges may be at the center of their academic storm, as they commonly are for countless other students on American campuses. Removed from their daily lives, and respectful of their independence, what can you do?

- *Know what resources the college offers.* Any university or college with a residential program will have a health center, a counseling center for mental health, and a dining program. All of these are led by professionals in their field, dedicated to student health and success. Even if they can't talk to you about your child's specific situation (to respect US federal privacy laws), they can explain their services and procedures. They can point you to parenting resources and literature to help you understand the situation. And they can provide reassurance that your son or daughter is in good hands.

- *Urge your student to take advantage of them.* If you feel shame or embarrassment that your child needs help, it's time to get over that. You need to show leadership and resolve here, helping them to see the value of getting support and taking advantage of key services, such as counseling and health monitoring. Visiting the counseling center for emotional therapy should be no different than visiting a doctor when you have a broken ankle. You need to send the signals or state outright that it's OK to do that. "Get help when you need help or even if you're unsure" should be your message.

- *Talk to your son or daughter about their health.* This guidebook is all about initiating open conversations between you and your student. I've counseled that you should initiate conversations as gently and without judgment as you can. The conversation about health is more important than any other, and you have a right to be concerned, of course. So it is appropriate to talk to them about how they are, how they are feeling, whether they are eating and sleeping well, and what challenges they are facing in all of these. Gauging their mood, their focus, and their attitude is important, though I know it is difficult from a distance. Inasmuch as too much communication interferes with their growth as an adult, you can temper that model with concerns about their health. And urge them to make it their highest priority.

A Note about Withdrawing and Transferring

Your daughter or son may have so many challenges, and so many poor grades, that they are asked to leave the university or college. At Johns Hopkins University, students below a 2.0 (or C) average are put on probation for a semester and required to seek assistance from Academic Advising and other services. If they do not improve their performance, they would be withdrawn for a semester. At the end of that period, they apply for reinstatement, write a letter that outlines what went wrong, what they will do to change, and what are their plans for a more successful future.

No one wants to go through this. Professors don't want to give failing grades any more than students want to get them. Advisors and deans do their best to be flexible and fair. But sometimes it is best to step away when you are failing, to regroup and recalibrate. No athlete can recover from a major injury and compete at the same time. And no student can both cope with real challenges, such as clinical depression or the loss of a parent, while studying for calculus and chemistry.

Dozens of students that I worked with at Hopkins were told to leave, and they returned stronger and more focused. They came to see that significant corrections were needed and that their college education was too important to take lightly or without addressing distractions and illness.

Your job is to suffer in silence. You may feel anger, disappointment, humiliation, and dishonor. You will feel the embarrassment of crafting a story for neighbors to explain why your daughter is home when she should be at school. But these feelings are not for sharing with your child. Talk to someone else. See your own therapist. Pray, work out, or yell into a pillow.

You need to refocus on the diagnosis of the problem, which may be of your doing if you have forced choices on your student that don't fit. And you need to deploy resources, medical and emotional, that help them regroup, recover, and forgive themselves. You are the adult here, and that role is lousy. But that's sometimes what parents have to do.

Your family may consider that transferring to a new college or university is one of those solutions. I would make this decision carefully and hesitantly. Transferring can appear to be a simple solution to a complex set of problems. It is possible, of course, that being closer to home or going to a college with smaller classes would help a great deal.

But problems may follow your daughter or son, particularly if they are emotional and motivational. Feeling the sting of failure is difficult, and a new location can help a student start afresh. But afresh is not like changing your clothes.

You already know that the plan has been blown. Your son or daughter is not going to take the courses you expected. They are not going to graduate when you had hoped. They are not having the great time that you may have had in college. And you will have to struggle with your own feelings about what went wrong and what role you played.

Try to take a breath and forgive yourself. Set aside your stake in this drama, and focus on what they need to move forward. I wish you all the best.

Around the Kitchen Table

Recovering from mistakes, disasters, and problems—both of our making and out of our hands—is one of life's great challenges. Your daughter or son will face this challenge throughout their lives. College offers a safe place to grow up and to transition to adulthood in many ways. So it is an ideal opportunity to learn how to recover, building on skills you have helped them develop all their lives. From learning how to walk to recovering from disappointing SAT scores, they have consistently bounced back—and you have supported that.

Now you have to figure out how to be supportive of an adult, not a child. They have not made it all the way to adulthood yet. But if you think of them as adults worthy of your respect and encouragement, rather than as children who need a strong hand, you are creating new expectations for them and a new way to define your relationship.

The conversations I've suggested in this chapter should be done gently, with adulthood in mind. Conversations should start with questions that are less loaded and direct than you are accustomed to. You know the stakes are high; they have been tripped by failure and may be in a serious moment of choice. But you will not get them back on track by force. Gentle conviction that they can succeed, warm confidence that they have what they need to recover, and strong support for any resources they need—that is your blend of strategies for recovery.

I nearly forgot to finish the story of your daughter at the foul line.

Standing there, she bounces the basketball a few more times than usual, hoping this moment will go away. Then she looks into the nervous but encouraging eyes of her teammates. She hears your voice of confidence over the crowd, and her coach's distinctive clapping. She remembers to breathe, helping her regain focus. She looks to the rim and realizes she has practiced this many times. She lets the ball go, it flies a little off center, rolls around the rim, and . . .

Goes in.

➡️ * You have been having a really tough time. What do you need from me and the college to help you? Can you give me some examples?
   * I'm betting it's hard to get motivated for courses that seem boring or that are giving you a hard time. Are you feeling that way? Do you have any ideas for how to find a better way?
   * What do you know about the resources on campus? Your resident assistant, academic advisor, college dean? Do you know about the tutoring center? Do they have a study assistance program?
   * How do you feel about those resources? What would hold you back from using them?
   * How does your professor offer to help? Have you tried their office hours? Does that seem intimidating? How might you make that easier to do?
   * What have you heard about why other kids are struggling? Does anyone you know seem depressed or really troubled? Does that seem familiar to you?
   * Are you OK? You have seemed really unhappy to me. Can I help? Do you want to talk about it? Would it be better to talk to someone else? Do you need any suggestions for who that might be?
   * You need to understand that I love you. I want you to be happy. And I want you to learn how to forgive yourself when you struggle and make mistakes. Do you understand that?

Encourage Them to Plan for Life after College

While I was a professor at the UCLA Center for American Politics and Public Policy in Washington, DC, I discovered that my students worried a great deal about their professional futures. Every grade contributed to a record to prove their worth. Every course was a stepping-stone to impress employers or graduate schools. Every relationship with professors could result in a good letter of recommendation. And they chose majors as part of an inexorable path to a specific profession.

I'm probably overstating this. My students were unusual, traveling to Washington, DC, to take courses and integrate an internship with original research. They mostly wanted to become lawyers, and we began a series of friendly arguments over that choice. "You can do almost anything with a law degree," they would say. "I suppose," I would counter, "but they're training to practice law. They can do almost anything because they're smart, not just because they're lawyers."

They often mistook my skepticism for opposition to their plans. I tried to reassure them that the problem was not the choice of the law. The problem was that their choice was often a lazy one, shaped by rumor and half-baked thinking about what law school and the practice of law was like. Lawyers make money, and the profession carried prestige, they argued. But that didn't mean it was a good fit for them.

Indeed, I found out that they had invented their college careers at UCLA backward. Rather than taking political sciences courses because the content was interesting, they took them to satisfy the perception that law schools want political scientists. They worked hard for grades not because they wanted to learn and internalize the material, but to boost a GPA in a tough law school admissions environment. This struck me as all wrong and unsustainable, a theory later confirmed by 10 years of advising at Johns Hopkins University.

Talking to students in the UCLA-Washington program launched my career in advising, in fact. I have since become convinced that pre-professional thinking dominates the choices of most students, though I cannot quantify that. So I could have started this guidebook with this final chapter, Strategy #10, *Encourage Them to Plan for Life after College*. But I want to end this guidebook with a conversation that you can have with your son or daughter about how careers, or more accurately, the perception of careers affects their decision-making.

What Do You Want to Be When You Grow Up?

Let's start with this innocent question. As your kids grew up, you may have posed this question to them many times. Adult friends and relatives likely did the same, both out of curiosity and to show the child that they were interested in their lives. On one level, this is a perfectly harmless question. It can provoke fun fantasies of being an astronaut, a fireman, or the goalie for the Women's World Cup champion. It helps children think about the world beyond in ways that can be reassuring and exciting. Who wouldn't want to save lives or score the winning run of the World Series?

But the question is problematic, and you need to consider this as you have conversations with your student about their college experience. As she or he ages, your child may begin taking this question more seriously. That may be natural, as life after college is coming with stern certainty.

That can be combined, as I have found with many students, with a real or imagined obligation to answer the question. If "I want to be a doctor" becomes the frequent answer, for a series of both good and poorly conceived reasons, then it takes on an authority of its own. Pretty soon, everyone is assuming this is the plan, and all the academic choices fall in line, even though the answer wasn't meant as a contract.

You need to think about this as you initiate or participate in conversations about careers. Where did the plan come from? How serious was it meant to be? Have we been asking what they do to reassure ourselves or to prompt optimistic thinking? Who is served by the answer? Is there another way to ask questions about their future? Or should you encourage them to say, "I don't know"?

Let Them Embrace Uncertainty

You and your child both want reassurance about the future. It's a scary place. That's why students love to have a plan, an answer to the uncertainty of a murky and distant future. "I don't know" to the question about careers seems both lame and without confidence. But like a lot of confident answers to complex questions, bravado is likely covering meaningful doubt and worry.

I suggest a more direct approach, one that can open a conversation about your shared worries. How about, "*How* are you thinking about life after college?" You can mean that literally, focused on *how* they are thinking rather than *what* they are thinking. By focusing on process, you're asking them to tell you what they are considering, why they are weighing one choice over another, and what models they might be following—including yours. This opens up a much more meaningful conversation in which the outcome is reassurance that they have *started* a process of decision-making, a process in its infancy and subject to many changes in the years ahead.

In other words, you are telling them indirectly (though you can outright) that it's OK to be uncertain, that there is much they can't know yet, and that they can in the short run just focus on making the most of their college experience. As I argue in *Dean's List*, career uncertainty is a modern luxury, a hard-fought freedom given this generation by waves of ancestors who did not have their choices. Your ancestors, like mine, especially the women of our families, did not choose to be farmers, laborers, grocers, carpenters, housekeepers. That choice was made for them. Perhaps there was some comfort in knowing their fate, but I'll bet any of them would trade that for the uncertainty and wide choices of today's college student.

A Plan to Have a Plan

Some students listen to the argument on the joys of uncertainty and then happily resign themselves to indecision and inaction. "Great," they say, "I can just let the future come." And then they move back into your house after graduation.

Let me be clearer, then. Knowing the future is uncertain is not an excuse for laziness. It is an explanation for anxiety. Even better, it is an invitation to experiment. But it doesn't get your daughter or son off the hook entirely. In fact, uncertainty offers a challenge to your student, one they can address with the kind of discipline and hard work that they put into choosing a college.

I have always been mystified by college students who do not use the Career Center on their campus. This place is packed with resources tailored for their needs—interest and skills assessment tools, alumni contacts, search tools for jobs and internships, workshops on every challenge in the search process, and of course counselors who know the student body and how to guide a college student. All included in the price. Yet students continue to think of the center as a place to format a resumé if you want to become an investment banker. Otherwise, forget it.

You can do two things in this complicated mix of anxiety, denial, and laziness. First, you can ask whether they know about and have taken advantage of those resources. As usual, I will suggest you do this gently, as any conversation about the uncertain future is going to provoke further anxiety and resentment.

You should acknowledge their feelings, reminding them that the college search they just completed was scary. Those fears went away as they learned about their specific choices for college, figured out what was important to them, and used data (such as GPA/SAT tables) to see where they might enjoy success. Following a structured process of career discovery, using campus resources, such as a Career Center, can give them the same sense of structure and control that they felt while choosing a college.

The second conversation you can try is to recount your own professional journey. There may be significant differences if you did not go to college, if you're a foreign national, or if you made choices that just don't make sense to your students (if you're, say, an engineer and they like the arts). But you may find that admitting to your own early confusion, mistakes, and uncertainty will ease whatever pressure they may feel from you.

You can share how you took stock of what was interesting or important. Or that you didn't do that, and wished you had. You could explain how you made careful choices. Or that you didn't, and wished you had. You could explain that you miscalculated or failed. Or maybe things went well.

I look back at my own early career and wonder why I didn't get any help. I just ricocheted from one idea to another without any discipline or data to shape my thinking. Maybe you were as sloppy as I was. Either way, these stories make uncertainty more normal, and they can make your gentle advice to get help more legitimate and understandable. You aren't lecturing to them, you're sharing experiences.

Supporting Their Graduate School Plans

Conversations about careers often lead to the tentative conclusion that going to graduate school is a good idea. My UCLA students knew I was skeptical about law school, but I obviously knew that they couldn't be lawyers without attending one. Let's set aside the question about whether going to graduate or professional school makes sense, and talk about how you can support them if they make that choice. Some suggestions:

- *Tell them it's powerful to be unique.* Graduate schools assemble classes, just as colleges do, so they look to construct a diverse group. Of course, their admitted students have to be qualified, with academic records that show ability and expertise. That's obvious, but parents can get stuck there, thinking that GPA is all that matters. From the graduate school's perspective, they get plenty of students who surpass whatever standards they have set, allowing them to construct a class with many interests, personalities, and ambitions. Admission committees need to satisfy many needs, such as the demands of diverse faculty members to match students with their interests. This means students can be strong in choosing academic programs that suit their own needs and talents, creating a unique profile that graduate schools admire—just because that profile is different.

- *Encourage them to put distance between them and the competition.* Again, this is not a matter of a higher GPA, though I won't dispute the advantages of that. An application should have "pop" to stand out, which requires taking what is unique and pushing it further. For example, if they love their cognitive science classes, how about a research experience on the effects of alcohol on memory? If they have a talent for civil engineering, how about working on a construction site or assisting a relative who repairs elevators? If they are interested in medical school, but prefer to major in a humanities discipline, how about connecting that discipline—say, music theory—to a medical challenge, such as music therapy for clinical depression. It's important that you understand I am not suggesting you make their fundamental choices, such as what to study. I'm advising that you help them magnify what is best, true, and unique about them. Invite them to be creative with what they love, not resentful with a choice they can't embrace.
- *Don't set the table for cheating.* In the first edition of *Dean's List*, I spent a lot of time lecturing my student readers about the dangers of cheating. I found that heavy-handed, so I dropped it. But I will warn you here that academic cheating can destroy a student's chance of admission to a good graduate school. She or he will have to report any conviction of cheating, which likely is noted on the transcript anyway. I don't recommend that you lecture your student about cheating itself, largely because it's probably too late to do that. Cheating can result from the very pressures you may be fueling by demands for a specific course of study or grades at the highest level. If your son or daughter is taking courses mostly to satisfy your expectations or the plan that you invented, they are likely to suffer from disinterest and resentment. Uninterested in their studies, they fall behind and begin getting poor grades. To pull those grades, they may think that cheating is their best—or even their only—choice. If you make it clear that they need to make their own choices and get help from professors, teaching assistants, and tutors when they need it, you are creating a dynamic that lessens the possibility of cheating.

Support a Short-Term Solution

What happens when all of this doesn't work? What do you do if they're threatening to move home, without direction, without a plan, without a job, without admission to graduate school? This can be a difficult moment, filled with disappointment and even shame. You may voice the dark feeling that the college experience was a bust. You might complain that the choices they made did not pay off, leaving them with a worthless college degree.

Please don't do that.

It will not help the family dynamic, it will not put the worth of college in the proper light, and it will not solve any needs other than the cold comfort of venting anger and anxiety. That is no solution here, in the short or long run.

There are some happier, more useful alternatives:

• *It's never too late for counseling.* While they may not live on campus any longer, most colleges extend counseling and networking privileges to graduates. Counseling—along with the self assessment and structured analysis that comes with it—is always helpful. Having moved home, your son or daughter may finally realize that they should have done this kind of disciplined thinking while in college. But you can gently point out there's still time to get help.

• *Remind them of their instinct to serve.* Most college students I have known don't have the foresight or experience to choose a lifelong career—if such a thing exists in a modern economy. Thinking they need this guidepost in place, they feel lost when it's not there. So you may want to remind them, if it's true, that serving others has been an important part of their lives. Perhaps they volunteered in a soup kitchen or retirement community while in high school. Maybe they tutored local children in the neighborhood next to the college, or their sorority or fraternity had many charity events. In the short run, without a career in mind, they can serve others. There are terrific, life-changing programs such as the Peace Corps, AmeriCorps, and Teach for America. They may not solve the problem of what to do with their professional lives, but these experiences give young people a chance to do something meaningful, admirable, and responsible while they try to figure it out.

- *Support the invitation to travel.* Most people can't afford to strap on a backpack after graduation and wander the world for months. But the call to explore is powerful for young people, perhaps because they know that such exploration will quickly get out of reach if they start a family or return to school. Do what you can to support this, if they hear this call. While you may be reluctant to fund anything after years of tuition payments, maybe you could split the cost of airfare to a destination where in-country travel is cheap: Eastern Europe, South America, Africa, or South Asia. Or have them look at available grants, such as the Fulbright Scholarship. My year in India, just after college, on a Fulbright changed my life forever, giving me the most provocative, memorable educational experience ever. You don't have to be an enrolled student to apply for a Fulbright. They go all over the world, varying in competition by country, and can fund research, public service, and, especially, teaching English.

- *Let them have some time.* If you can keep your anxieties and even anger under control, you may be forgiving enough to let them have some time and even some fun. You likely would prefer that they didn't move back home, particularly if they seem to been wasting time and exploiting your hospitality. Try a little patience here, knowing that college could have been very intense and even exhausting. But give this a little structure, purpose—and a deadline. Suggest they move to a place that promises an exciting life for a young person, like a major city where they have many college friends. It may not be ideal, but if they can support themselves somehow, and learn the challenges of adulthood, they may come to the conclusion that they need to figure out their first professional steps beyond a Starbucks barista. Rushing to graduate school, without a sense of what awaits on the far side, is not a good solution to indecision. It can saddle them with debt and with expectations that may not meet their long-term needs. Don't add to the pressure to make a premature decision.

Around the Kitchen Table

Parenting is pretty unforgiving, as life keeps challenging our children with new obstacles. As those obstacles change, our children grow and our role keeps shifting. Making sure our children become self-sufficient and happy adults is, I suppose, our primary role. Everything feeds into it, from how we bond with them as babies, to how we hope to make them stronger every day with good food, a rich education, and a loving environment. Positioning them to fly after college is a worthy goal, but it is filled with anxiety caused by all the uncertainties that life after college presents.

I have argued that these uncertainties color decisions throughout a student's college life, but there is a way to navigate out of this. The simple solution, frankly, is to lighten up. A college student has enough anxieties about the future without having to handle yours, too. You are not doing them a favor, nor offering any real solutions, by channeling your worries and guilt into pressured expectations on them.

When you cling to an idea—they must be a doctor or an engineer—as an easy solution to your own need to stop thinking about how secure they will be professionally, you create a cascade of problems. They follow this path with resentment and ultimate failure, or they intentionally defy your plan and end up with equally poor alternatives.

Look, I'm terrified, too. I have no idea what my son in college is going to do with his life. But I keep trying to remember that it is *his* life. He needs to own his choices and take his path, however worried I might be about it. He will only be happy if those choices are his, not mine. I can make good suggestions—be disciplined in your thinking, thorough in your research, open-minded in exploring options, get help even if you don't think you need it, have patience in letting the future arrive—but, ultimately, I will have to let go and hope for the best.

➡ * What do you think when someone asks, "What will you do when you grow up?"
* How does it feel when I ask you about your plans after college?
* Does life after college worry you? Can you think of ways to help you be less worried about it?

* What are your friends thinking about? Does it help or hurt to know that and why?
* What kind of help could you get to work on this? Does anyone use the Career Center? Why not?
* Let's think short term, not forever. Can you think of some things to do for a few years after graduating?
* I really think that graduate school is different than college. College helps you explore the world and yourself. Graduate school gives you tools for a specific job. Without knowing the job or the path, how can you choose a program? Would you agree with that or not? Why or why not?
* Other than me, who is pressuring you on your career choices? Do you have a way to push back?
* What do you think will make you happy? If you don't know, maybe you should think about that as hard as you did about colleges. Does that make sense?

Conclusion

Final Thoughts

This guidebook has offered you a journey through the many challenges of supporting a college student, who will be on his or her own journey of discovery, perhaps guided by *Dean's List*. I hope that it has offered you and your daughter or son the chance to walk that journey side by side, in healthy, structured, and productive conversations. I've given you many questions to support those conversations. Some of them, particularly when failure is the topic, will be difficult.

I have been on my own journey in writing it over the course of my older son's first year at Dickinson College. I have learned, as I hope you will, to remain calm and confident while his life unfolded far from our home. I came to accept that my role was secondary to his successful year of studies and activities. I couldn't see what was happening, and worrying about it became increasingly pointless—if it ever had purpose. I stopped texting so much or wondering whether I was texting too much. And I learned something obvious: As a college administrator it is easy to find fault with parents who interfere and intervene. As a parent, I now get it.

So I have tried to find a middle way that I hope you will find useful as you discover a role that suits you and helps you support your student to a rich and successful college experience. There is no need to fully detach yourself, but you must respect their need for distance and to own their decisions. You can offer advice, from suggesting they get to know professors to getting career counseling, but you will have to accept that your advice may be met with resentment. That is why I have repeatedly used the word *gently*. Good, quiet, balanced advice will get traction if delivered without insistence, anger, impatience, or dominion.

If you use a delicate hand in supporting your daughter or son, they should forgive your involvement, and you will be giving them the room and discretion to make choices they can own and take adult responsibility for making. If you push too hard, even with the right intentions, the relationship can blow up and you can lose the opportunity to influence their success.

I now understand, and I hope you do, too, that this balance is hard to achieve and ever-changing. Give yourself some credit for trying to keep that balance, remaining supportive without being overbearing. Forgive yourself if you overstep, appreciating that it's hard to know what overstepping means when the line keeps shifting. Learn to listen more and talk less, as listening will give you a more accurate read on that line, and you will show them that you respect their choices, opinions, and voice.

Most of all, remain confident that your own choices and words are guided by love.

Good luck and Godspeed.

INDEX

grades (continued)
consequences of, 16–17, 86; parent oversight, 25; pleasing instructors, 17; power of, 16; zero-sum game, 18

health concerns, 9, 28–29, 91–92, 103
high school: differences with college, 9, 34, 35, 63–64, 65, 88, 100; graduation, 13
Hupart, Marvin, 8

lectures, 66–68

majors, 6, 53–54, 60–61; and academic failure, 59–60, 97; choosing, 57–60; and practicality, 58; and relation with careers, 54–55; role and meaning, 55–56
mental health, 29, 91–92
Millennials, 4, 26

parenting: and academic failure, 84–85, 92–93, 96–99, 104–6; being supportive, 9; changing roles, 2, 5, 8, 30–32, 33, 50–51, 63–64, 68, 71, 81–82, 117–18; "helicopter parents," 3–4, 24; important conversations, 2–3, 7, 11, 56, 71, 84–85, 92–93, 99, 105–6, 109, 110–11; independent decision making, 3, 28, 31, 32, 60–61, 69–70, 87; letting go, 3, 11, 24; modesty, 8; role in college applications, 25; role in course selection, 26–27, 44–45, 50–51; role in health issues, 69–70, 91–92; role in studying, 26, 63–64; student that move back home, 113–14; and uncertainty, 115
pre-law planning, 107–8
pre-medical education, 47, 55, 87, 112
procrastination, 87, 88, 99–100
program directors, 41
provosts, 42

resident assistants, 40–41

service options, 113
sleep, 70–71
study abroad, 79–82; costs of, 81; and safety, 80
study habits, 6, 63–64; note taking, 68; productivity, 69–70; strategic approach to, 64–66; and "study consulting," 66, 101
success, definition of, 9–10, 13–14, 15, 19–20

teaching assistants, 36, 41, 67
time management, 88–89
transferring colleges, 104–5
tuition as investment with "pay off," 14

US colleges, history of, 19–20

why go to college, 4, 98–99

About the Author

John Bader served Johns Hopkins University in several deanships from 2001 to 2011, including Associate Dean for Undergraduate Academic Affairs and Assistant Dean of Academic Advising. He also coached students as the university's National Scholarships Advisor. These experiences inspired and informed this guidebook and its companion, *Dean's List: 10 Strategies for College Success.* He is also author of *Taking the Initiative: Agenda Setting in Congress and the "Contract with America."* He is now Executive Director of the Fulbright Association, the official alumni organization of the scholarship. Prior to his tenure at Johns Hopkins University, he was Director of Washington Programs and Assistant Professor of Political Science for the UCLA Center for American Politics and Public Policy. His unusual career also has included teaching history in public schools (including his own high school), working in the Political Unit at ABC News, and serving as Policy Director for Jon Corzine's successful US Senate campaign in 2000. He earned a BA in history from Yale University and a MA and a PhD in political science from the University of Wisconsin–Madison. He was a Fulbright Scholar to India and a Governmental Studies Graduate Fellow at the Brookings Institution. He received the inaugural Global Changemaker Award from the Institute of International Education in 2016. He and his wife, Amy, are the delighted parents of Calvin and Eli.